DIRECTIONS

A Look at the Paths of Life

DIRECTIONS
A Look at the Paths of Life

Walter R. L. Scragg

Southern Publishing Association
Nashville, Tennessee

Dedication

To my wife,
BETTY

Contents

Contents

Directions

You seldom see them now. But just a few years back another generation of bearded youth roamed the hinterland. Escapees from the humdrum, dropouts from the treadmill, we knew them as "swaggies."

Australia immortalizes its tramps in the song "Waltzing Matilda." Swagmen humped their swags and went "waltzing Matilda" along the roads and tracks of the outback. No time clocks, routines, or appointments marred their errant bliss.

Along the dirt and gravel roads of the inland they could be seen: not hitchhiking (all those gates to open!), just waltzing in the summer's blue haze.

Ambling a way from one sheep station to the next might take a day or even two. A night might have to be spent camped by a billabong (bayou), defeating mosquitoes with a smoky fire. But a birdcall rising would thwart the heat of the day, and an evening stroll bring one close to a benevolent station owner whose kindly heart assured a bed and supper, with only a modicum of work in payment.

At another sunset in another generation the hoboes of today meander their way through life. Twice as

Directions

I have window-shopped near the intersection of Hollywood and Vine in Los Angeles, sweet young ladies have blocked my path. Barefooted, serape-clad, all smiling innocence, both requested whimsically, "Excuse me, could you give me a nickel?"

They were neither from the starving millions of India nor from the minions of immorality. One offered a reason.

With a glance at her friend a few feet off in the shadows she grinned, "We wanted to see your reaction. We do it for kicks."

Marginally better than phone-booth stuffing and decidedly an improvement on tire slashing, yet withal a fingerpost for directionless living.

Aimlessness inherits a long history. Greek philosophers deplored the idle of their day. The Middle Ages had its footloose wanderers. Today offers no surprises when it produces its own brand of drifters. For many, life doesn't seem to lead anywhere. Then why not squeeze it dry of fun, roister it with thrills day and night?

Yet life cries for definition. Even the most vagabond of wanderers will yield the concession that where you are going outranks where you are.

One hobo answered the question "How do you decide where to go next?" with an immortal, "I always walk with the wind at my back."

One of my first ventures into sailing put me aboard a fast Hobie catamaran. The run before the breeze exhilarated. Then came the moment to change direction. Try as I might I could not bring that craft around. Finally I jumped overboard in the shallows to try and manhandle her around. But the wind kept pulling the boat and me after it. It seemed smart to climb back on board, except that when I leaned on the rudder bar, it snapped. Now the boat yawed and bucked before the wind at will. Only a passing motorboat rescued me and the yacht from disaster against the piles of a nearby bridge.

Dreamers of man's future in space extrapolate streams of particles that traverse the ether like galactic Gulf Streams. They conjecture a spaceship driving before these space winds as a yacht before a wind.

From Columbus to Colonel Glenn, success has depended on direction. And that's as true spiritually as it is physically. A schooner dismasted in a storm is no more a tragedy than a life blown willy-nilly, out of control.

Faith for Today, asked Motivation Dynamics, a New York-based firm, to do an in-depth analysis of its television viewers and Bible students. Prime reason for seeking the hope nascent in the mix of the revered Word of God and the magic of the mass media was a sense of loss of purpose and direction to life. They came to the telecast seeking a guide, a way, a goal. They could remember the clarity and certainty of youth. They remembered when right was right and wrong was wrong, and they knew the difference. Now the edges of morality had blurred and eroded. They reached out for direction.

In seeking direction, some lives set phony goals. Row the Atlantic, or drift over it hanging from a balloon; swim the English Channel faster than anyone else; build a four-bedroom house with two and a half baths in seventy-five hours. As publicity stunts they're pretty good; as substitutes for a purpose in life they're a dead loss.

But let's not kid ourselves. It isn't easy to decide

on direction in life. The future flies off in all directions. Choices beckon this way and that. Of course, advice comes easily. A wife will offer one piece of advice, a teacher another, a counselor a third, and all too often the wise people don't agree.

This seems to make the words of Jesus particularly relevant: " 'I am the way, the truth, and the life; no one goes to the Father except by me' " (John 14:6, TEV).

Space bristles with complexities for its pilots. Which is up? Where is down? How far is here from there? And at what angle? Am I yawing? Is the ship rolling or pitching? What is the speed of rotation?

Inner space offers the same prickly complexity. That's why Jesus says, "I know the way. I can plot the coordinates. I can bring you to My Father. I know the direction—follow Me."

As I write this we are reading the reports of the Pioneer 10 flyby of Jupiter. Now its orbit has whipped it on its way to Saturn. Soon we'll know more about the queen of planets. All the planning is paying off in a welter of information about Jupiter and soon about its sister planet.

Out of college and university days comes a tossed salad of impressions. We rush-houred through logic; bypassed religion wherever possible; freewayed past exits marked with the names of great thinkers; read the signs marked with the titles of the great classics of human thought. In the struggle to systematize thought they frequently took the same turnpike we did. They left God out of the equation. They projected new direction for humanity—at times they even took man out of the equation. True, Plato had his Ideal; Nietzsche, his Superman; Marx, his Dialectic Materialist, but they are as far removed from the real man as the stars from each other.

To follow and accept Christ's suggestion would be to say that life blows steadily in the direction of God. No ship is lost whose rudder is Godward set. That's why the wisest of all could look at education and urge, "Wisdom is the principal thing; therefore get wisdom: and with all thy getting get understanding" (Proverbs 4:7, KJV). And, "the fear of the Lord is the beginning of wisdom: and the knowledge of the holy is understanding" (Proverbs 9:10, KJV). Somewhere in the gales of knowledge that shriek around our heads in the late teens and early twenties we need to know this truth and to set our sails accordingly.

Emile Coue, a psychotherapeutist, thought to give direction to the lives of his disciples and patients with the maxim "Every day in every way I am getting better and better." Jean-Paul Sartre urged consideration of the primacy of self within the given moment. And volumes of Plato, Zoroaster, Aristotle, Buddha, Muhammad, and numberless sages—ancient and modern—tout their own special "thing" about life.

Listen to Paul talking about God's new people: "When anyone is joined to Christ he is a new being; the old is gone, the new has come" (2 Corinthians 5:17, TEV). Hope has dawned eternally for humanity's thinkers that they can create a new race through new ideas. A philosopher is basically a shoestring man; he sees us lifting ourselves higher and higher by our own efforts. The course of the race rests in the human hand that guides the rudder.

Even when admitting the problems of depraved and stupid mankind, the philosopher offers the human solution. In *Walden Two* the behaviorist Burrhus

F. Skinner skirts the problems of depravity by a Utopian concept that pits the well-trained savant against the rest of humanity which needs his conditioning skills.

The Bible solves it a different way: "All this is done by God, who through Christ changed us from enemies into his friends" (2 Corinthians 5:18, TEV). The Bible says change is possible. A new direction lies always at the doorstep of all men.

That's why being a Christian is different. The uncertainty has gone. Direction is assured. We know why we are here, we know where we are going. With that direction comes change.

The real butterfly does not crawl through life gobbling leaves and garbage. The real butterfly bursts the chrysalis and spreads beautiful wings in the sun. Do not imagine that how you now know yourself is how you are meant to be. Under the influence of Christ the ugliness of self sloughs off to reveal self as God meant it to be, a likeness to the Son of God Himself.

The transformation in Christ sometimes surprises us with the values it brings. Enid Haupt of *Seventeen* writes, "I don't think there is a 'new morality.' I believe most young people are searching today for less hypocrisy and more honesty, for a better code of ethics, and for those values for which this country has always stood but which they feel are lacking today" (*Advertising Age*, March 2, 1970, p. 12). A Christian could hardly argue with this statement.

Commenting on attitudes toward love, Haupt says, "They speak less of love. The terms are now 'meaningful' or 'real' relationships. Young people feel a deeper emotional bond than the word *love* connotes to them. Young people want to like the person that they love. So their relationship is a companionable one as well" (*ibid.*, p. 17).

Read 1 Corinthians 13. See how closely Christianity's values match the modes of many moderns.

An authority asserts itself in the direction of God's new people. They walk with surefootedness through the bogs of lust and passion. "This is how we win the victory over the world: with our faith. Who can defeat the world? Only he who believes that Jesus is the Son of God" (1 John 5:4, 5, TEV).

God's new people never walk with the wind at their back. It isn't that easy. They cannot "do their own thing" and walk off willingly with the crowd. For them there are moments of evaluation, a reference to the authority Christ brings to their lives, a resetting of course, and then a sure step forward.

The pines of Cape Cod illustrate our point. In the valley they stand straight and tall. Where the sand dunes rise, the green foliage contrasts as with snow. But the same pines suffer at the thrust of the prevailing wind. On the coastal ridges they lie close to the ground, hugging contours away from the wind—a scraggy caricature of their brothers of the valley.

For a life to grow to its perfection, it needs the shelter of Christ's life. The gales of habit, circumstances, opinion, bend every life away from Him.

Yet there is the other wind that blows toward God, pointing life upward and straight toward the Sun of righteousness. It blows with the influence and power of the Spirit of God. Sheltered, transformed, directed—that's the promise of the new people God makes every day.

When Jesus said, "I am the way," He said it all. He is *the* Direction of life.

Nobody Else Exactly Like You

The camera closes on a lady using body English to guide her bowling ball toward the pins. A golfer putts, and as the ball slides into the cup he exults with a high kick. Freeze frame. Voice over: "There's nobody else exactly like you."

Thus television makes another succinct contribution to the wisdom of the human race. Equitable Life, which spawned this gem, has it right. Though theology hardly lies within their expertise, the insurance company told it better for God than just about anyone else ever did. Chalk up one for Madison Avenue.

Only Western culture could breed a slogan like that. And Western thinking found this idea in the Bible. The Bible never lets up on the theme of the uniqueness and individuality of all people.

How alike can people be? During the summer of 1974 the news media had a day off from Watergate and concentrated on the saga of Clara and Alta Rodriguez. Born attached to each other at abdomen and pelvis, the thirteen-month-old Siamese twins faced a ten-and-a-half-hour operation as surgeons disconnected them.

When the feats of creating a new colon and rectum for one child and stitching up the huge wounds in both abdomens ended, the babies faced another threat even more serious than possible infection. For the first time they lay in separate cribs, and physicians feared that psychological trauma might cause shock and threaten their lives. At the first practical moment they were returned to the one crib to continue life together until they learned that they were two different people.

Yet, given time, the Dominican babies might have become individuals in their own right, even without the surgery. The original Siamese twins, who toured as vaudeville celebrities, developed into distinct individuals with their own tastes in clothes, food, activities, and sleeping patterns.

The mind boggles at the concept of four billion people all unique. Surely somewhere, characteristics must match perfectly. Yet genetic scientists assure us that they are all different. The probability of two people exactly alike lies outside the laws of chance.

That idea is not a comforting thought. We prefer our people arranged in orderly groups. India structured its castes; Britain, its classes; medieval Europe, its feudal orders.

To try and get it all in order we fall into various traps that hide a person's individuality from us. We categorize people—commies, red-necks, niggers, Jews, whities, the man, the establishment. If anyone shows the characteristics of one of these groups, we feel we can safely lump him or her along with the rest and dismiss the whole bunch. It's convenient, it's comforting, but it isn't Christian. It's not even sane. Such thinking has bred more oppression, more persecution, more exploitation, more wars, than any other human quirk.

The Bible does have a category for all men—sinners—but that never serves to hide the individual from God. Rather it becomes a spur to divine action as it seeks for the ones who will respond to the change Christ gives.

Adam and Eve carried within them the infinite genetic possibilities that make every person unique. Four billion haven't lessened the reservoir of differentness, nor will seven billion or even twenty billion.

This differentness holds opportunity for the Spirit of God. He can take you and make you into something no one else could ever be. He knows the potential of every human being and what might be accomplished with God helping.

At first glance Christianity doesn't seem to be that kind of religion. We sing, "Like a mighty army/ Moves the church of God." We hear the voice of Christ pleading, "that they all may be one." We read Paul's declaration, "one body, . . . one Spirit, . . . one hope, . . . one Lord, one faith, one baptism." The easy picture forms a uniformed army moving forward with robot precision under the banner of the King, wheeling and advancing at His command. And Christianity is partly that too. But if you think that the army is drafted in masses, you have it wrong.

When the Zaire government compelled certain small sects to join larger churches, many came to the Seventh-day Adventists. Memberships as high as 100,000 sought admission. Many of these people thought they could walk through the water and right on into the church. They thought the Adventists difficult because they indoctrinated and baptized one person on his stand rather than a whole church or denomination.

Another picture forms easily. We chant, "More and more like Jesus." We scale the heights of Christ-like manhood and womanhood, seeking always "to be like Him," as if the height of achievement is to lose identity and become like someone else.

But Christianity is not Hinduism or Buddhism. They hold out the goal of Nirvana where the soul finds oblivion in the oneness of the universe. They believe that to arrive at the goal is to be ignorant of that arrival, to discover God is to discover unconsciousness and know nothing of the discovery.

God does not march an army of puppets over the landscape of righteousness. He gives us the preposterous (by human thinking) notion that He counts the hairs of our heads.

Surrender to Christ kindles personal identity and reinforces it. Paul awoke to the wonder of being God's man and found himself enriched, fulfilled, empowered more than he had dreamed possible. By becoming God's person he tapped into batteries of power he did not know existed. He felt no lessening because, "in his good pleasure God, who had set me apart from birth and called me through his grace, chose to reveal his Son to me and through me, in order that I might proclaim him among the Gentiles" (Galatians 1:15, 16, NEB). He discovered that he could do all things through Christ, who strengthened him (Philippians 4:13).

"When the mind of man is brought into communion with the mind of God, the finite with the Infinite, the effect on body and mind and soul is beyond estimate. In such communion is found the highest education. It is God's own method of development" (E. G. White, *The Acts of the Apostles*, p. 126).

The explosion of the uniqueness that was Paul gave the world its greatest missionary and keenest theologian.

Paul knew the battle for nobility and character. He had lost out in the struggle time and again. In Christ he cried, "Miserable creature that I am, who is there to rescue me out of this body doomed to death?" Then and then only could he claim the victory and the release, "God alone, through Jesus Christ our Lord! Thanks be to God!" (Romans 7:24, 25, NEB).

I remember the confusion of the masses of India. I had no way of compassing what I saw. The trap opened and I found myself saying, "They all look alike to me." I found myself not even wanting to tell them apart. To do that would create personality for them, and personality would create relationship, and relationship would make responsibility. And responsibility for 500 million Indians I did not want. Even five thousand in one village loomed too large for me.

And God? Can He tell the difference from way out there? Has He turned the telescope of omniscience around so as to view us as a mass rather than as persons? We can concede it was easy for Him when all He had was Adam and Eve, but what about now?

This is not an exercise in egocentricity, and before we exalt our individual selves too much, let's remind ourselves that these are but "parts of His ways"—that there was a time when "the sons of God shouted for joy," and that ten thousand times ten thousand minister before Him.

And let's not forget that God both is and is not

way out there. After Jesus left, He gave us the Holy Spirit so that He might never be away from us. The Spirit is everyone's God. No one can hide from Him, and He hides from no one. Through Him Christ shines into every life. "The real light which enlightens every man was even then coming into the world" (John 1:9, NEB).

The Bible never hides man's potential or his problems behind a smear of generalizations or platitudes. Story after story recounts God's dealing with real people who have real names and real problems.

David trains himself to defend and provide for his stupid sheep. And for him that's about all life will ever be. God, who sees otherwise, challenges him with the taunts of the infidel Goliath, goads him with the assaults of the Philistines, and creates a king.

Moses squats at the feet of Egypt's wisest and best, acquits himself in the finest traditions of the Hebrew race, and prepares to be Israel's second Joseph in the service of the Pharaohs. He blunders—murders an Egyptian. Write "finis" for Moses. Not too soon though, God crafts the real Moses in the wilderness and gives the world one of its greatest intellects.

Peter arrives at his greatest ambition. He owns his fishing boat, his partners have skills that match his, his family surrounds him. He has it made. Then a Stranger calls, "Follow Me," and life is never the same again. Peter didn't know he had it in him, but God did. He saw the potential leader of the early church and set him free to do God's purposes.

We know we are different. The important thing is that God also knows: "God has laid a foundation, and it stands firm, with this inscription: 'The Lord knows his own' " (2 Timothy 2:19, NEB).

Directions

Something within us cries for a fresh start. Unwinding the past and projecting a different future lie beyond our reach, but we dream of them nonetheless. How can God make anything of lives whose decisions have moved away from Him? Can He take us from the many-branched trails of decision that we have followed thus far and lead us over new ground of His choosing?

Satan offers one solution. He continually touts evil as good. He gilds evil with pleasure. He tempts and deludes. The way seems good, but the end is damnation. One can't please the devil. He tempts to evil, then accuses us for being evil. Thus we slide ever downward.

God has a better idea. Not only does He offer the good life in Jesus Christ but He is also willing to take us where we are. He doesn't taunt; He takes hold and leads us out. We are never at a point from which we have to move before God takes over. Satan goads us to do better. Christ guides us into a better way.

Think about decisions for a moment. How many have made you what you are today? Some good decisions, some bad, some neutral. Years of decision without God. Years of decision in spite of God. Decisions of presumption, decisions of ignorance. We have followed the branching trail to this point, and where is the way to the person God wants us to be?

If you'd started earlier, it might be better; if you'd trusted more, it might be different. Who knows? And it doesn't matter with God. This is the starting point. This, now, is where we take off from. The God who knows His own is in control. Every moment of life of every individual on the face of the earth is a potential starting point. At this moment any one of the billions can reach out and take God's hand into the future.

A God-directed life isn't necessarily an escape from consequences. All too often our lives structure a mess from which we can never really escape. God knows these factors too. He's neither discouraged nor impressed by them. He feeds them into the computer of divine wisdom and devises the unique pattern of life that meets our capabilities and circumstances.

While we dream of what might have been, God will be wanting what might yet be. Then our role is cooperation, understanding, trust, faith.

Do you sometimes feel that you need Gideon's fleece to guide you down the way to God's future? If only we knew what God wanted us to do, what would be best for us, which decision to make, what a difference that would make to our lives!

While waiting for God to soak the fleece with dew, we may be overlooking the fleeces of God's promises. A Bible student once marked every promise he could find. Later he took time to test the promises of God and marked them with the letters TPT—tested and proved true. One by one he checked them off and decided that God meant every word He said. The Bible is full of Gideon's fleeces for us to know the way we should go.

And don't forget the guidance of the Holy Spirit. " 'He will guide you into all truth' " (John 16:13, KJV) —not only the true doctrine, but the truth about ourselves, the truth about God's will for us.

And when God has finished with you, who will you be?

"There are varieties of gifts, but the same Spirit.

There are varieties of service, but the same Lord. There are many forms of work, but all of them, in all men, are the work of the same God. In each of us the Spirit is manifested in one particular way for some useful purpose" (1 Corinthians 12:4-7, NEB). Note what God says He will do—"in each of us . . . in one particular way." There you are. God isn't going to make you into something you won't know as yourself. He's going to take the potential that is you and make you into something you'll wish you'd been all along.

The Spirit doesn't impose—He develops. He doesn't plant a guidance unit in us to automate our lives. He takes us for what we are and creates for us the "useful purpose" that was our intended destiny through Christ.

Oh, yes, sometimes He will give a miracle, or something so hidden within us that it seems a miracle. Like Ellen Harmon, age seventeen, hearing the Lord call her like Samuel of old. Yet even here the potential was there within the context of a life joined with Christ.

"One man, through the Spirit, has the gift of wise speech, while another, by the power of the same Spirit, can put the deepest knowledge into words. Another, by the same Spirit, is granted faith; another, by the one Spirit, gifts of healing" (verses 8, 9). Paul continues the list in 1 Corinthians 12, emphasizing that all the gifts come from "one and the same Spirit" (verse 11).

These are only samples from the Spirit. Talents and gifts form only part of the tools of the Spirit to create the developed Christian. He also has His fruits, His guidance, His prayers. His activity pervades the whole being of God's new people: character, personality, nature. And because we are different, He deals differently.

There's nobody else in the whole human race exactly like you. God made it that way; He wants it that way. Don't you wonder what surprises are in store in His future for you?

The
Do-It-Yourself
God Kit

The long features and sardonic grin result partly from the water-washed shape of the stone. The New Hebridean god from the island of Atchin adorns my office credenza. This was the way I thought it must be. When you want an idol, you go and find a stone, take your chisel, and set to work. I had even watched my Atchinese friend put the finishing touches on this little deity. After carving a god or painting his likeness, one could start right in and bedeck him with flowers, offer him food, or kneel and pray to him.

But in ancient India I learned something new about gods. One has to see the entrance to the Temple of a Thousand Pillars in Madurai to believe the variety and multitude of god-shapes possible. Four multi-storied towers mark each gate. Each has every niche and pilaster carved with gods.

Inside, gold glimmers from dusty corners. Altars mark the special attributes of pagan divinities. Obscene statues lurk in dark recesses. The more popular idols bear the patina of millions of hands. Kneeling blocks have darkened with the bowing of the faithful.

Priests hustle among the devotees, bowls of food appear from beneath robes, marigold perfume drifts from leis of fresh flowers.

As I watched, an Indian gentleman approached the altar of Ganesha, the benign human-elephant god. He dipped his fingers in ashes at the base of the image. Smearing the ashes on the forehead of the god, he transferred some to his own head. Finally he crossed his arms, pulled at the lobes of his ears three times in rapid succession, bowed toward the statue, and beat his fists against his temples. The rite over, he turned with a last bow toward the inner sanctum that the infidel Christian could only glimpse behind gold-woven curtains.

What did it mean?

He shrugged his ignorance. "It's what we do. It's the way to worship Ganesha."

A few minutes later I found the answer to a question that had been subliminally nagging at my consciousness all through my stay in the subcontinent. We paused to examine some skillfully executed images of Vishnu. Then as I turned to leave I noted diagrams on the wall. A whole series of them lined this remote corner of the temple. They were sketches of statues. In fact the whole thing was marked out like a blueprint.

My very first do-it-yourself god kit! Measurements to make a god by! Now I knew why a statue seen in Calcutta will repeat itself to the last detail in Cape Cormoran. Multiarmed Vishnu wasn't the result of free artistic imagination. Even each angle of the forty fingers had its diagram.

Just by following the instructions, anyone could carve his own Vishnu! Not that any Christian would ever want to build his own god! Holy statues for some, yes; sacred icons for others, yes; but gods? Never!

Ever so often skeptics revive the charge of anthropomorphism. Scanning the latest apologetic from Christian sources, they declare we are making God in our own image when He said we are made in His. If that is true, all of us have an inbuilt do-it-yourself godmaker. It's easier for us to make God like we want Him to be than to accept Him as He is.

When the cashier at the supermarket mentioned God, my ears probed for the conversation. She was talking to the packer.

"I went to a wedding down in Alabama last June. Some kind of Methodists. Do you know? They wouldn't have any dancing or drinking at the reception. Said it was sinful. Real hung up on this sin-bit."

The young man was a listener. "I know what you mean," he answered, noncommittally.

"But can you imagine it?" she bored on. "God —if you want to believe this God-bit—getting all uptight just because a few of us on old planet Earth want to jive around a little? He's got stars and planets and all that jazz out there. Why should He get all uptight about our having a good time down here?"

"I know what you mean." The youth sidled off to the next checkout.

"For thus says the high and lofty One who inhabits eternity, whose name is Holy: 'I dwell in the high and holy place, and also with him who is of a contrite and humble spirit, to revive the spirit of the humble, and to revive the heart of the contrite' " (Isaiah 57:15, RSV).

The Bible posits both the grandeur and the personalness of God. He is both transcendent and indwelling. He lives with man just as surely as He rules the universe. We cannot make Him be anything else.

History records the religious fanaticism and abuse of those who tried to manipulate God to their own purposes, those who sought to make God what they wanted instead of what He is. When Moses asked God His name, Jehovah replied, "I AM." This teaches that He is not only the eternal living God but also a God whose nature is determined and who will not be subject to man's pressures.

If God rules the universe and lives with the humble, then He compasses both the orbit of the stars and the dance hall in Alabama. His power sustains the universe, His love involves Him in the life of His created beings.

Two pictures display God's concern with small actions and unimportant people.

The oxcart jounces its way over the Judean hills. The sturdy pull of the yoked oxen keeps it astride the foot trail. A group of anxious men advance with the cart, keeping their distance, but wary for the fate of the cargo.

Suddenly a beast stumbles against a rocky outcrop. One man grabs for the box on the tray of the wagon. His hand touches the ark of the Ten Commandments. Uzzah screams and dies.

Already the Philistines had desecrated the sacred Testimony by placing it in their shrine. God had punished them for their presumption. Now Israel assumes too much and commits sacrilege. Uzzah's act challenges both the command of God concerning the ark and His promise to preserve a people for His name.

Directions

Mankind learns the lessons of presumption the hard way. No one manipulates God to his own ends. To transgress the direct will of the Lord is to presume as Lucifer presumed in heaven, or as Adam presumed in Eden. The penalty for presumptuous sin is death. Only Christ can remove that penalty, and even then the consequences may follow.

Eleven hundred years later Jesus Christ walks the trails of Judea. Because of His miracles, throngs crowd His every movement. On the edges of the multitude a woman pushes and strains her way nearer to the Healer.

She "had suffered terribly from severe bleeding for twelve years, even though she had been treated by many doctors. She had spent all her money, but instead of getting better she got worse all the time. She had heard about Jesus, so she came in the crowd behind him. 'If I touch just his clothes,' she said to herself, 'I shall get well.'

"She touched his cloak and her bleeding stopped at once; and she had the feeling inside herself that she was cured of her trouble. At once Jesus knew that power had gone out of him. So he turned around in the crowd and said, 'Who touched my clothes?'

"His disciples answered, 'You see how the people are crowding you; why do you ask who touched you?'

"But Jesus kept looking around to see who had done it. The woman realized what had happened to her; so she came, trembling with fear, fell at his feet, and told him the whole truth. Jesus said to her, 'My daughter, your faith has made you well. Go in peace, and be healed from your trouble' " (Mark 5:25-34, TEV).

God positions Himself in personal interaction

with man's needs. At times the thought comforts. At times it nettles. A God who interferes isn't such a pleasant thought to some people. A God who knows all things bothers others. So what to do? Get out the do-it-yourself god kit and make a god that suits our wishes? "God wouldn't do this. . . ." "God wouldn't concern Himself with such a small thing. . . ." "Surely that isn't important to God. . . ."

Just as bad is the thinking that excludes God from life's equations. "I'm not important enough for God to worry about. . . ." "I don't believe He hears me anyhow. . . ."

Yet all the time, the God who felt the touch of the woman's hand is waiting for your weak reaching toward Him. He is the God who can be touched. He is the God who touches. The personalness of God may be overlooked, but it never ceases to operate. And when we know Him for what He is, then we can submit and join Him in His quest for our best good.

The mind of divinity computes the alternates of the future from small acts, human decisions. As an electronic calculator will select the correct solution to a problem, He selects the best future that the choices of our lives leave open.

Only one release from sin exists—the blood of Jesus. "Ever since God created the world, his invisible qualities, both his eternal power and his divine nature, have been clearly seen. Men can perceive them in the things that God has made. So they have no excuse at all!"(Romans 1:20, TEV).

One can't excuse a bad temper on inheritance or circumstance. A murder is no less culpable because of the hate or anger that flares momentarily. A theft still ranks as dishonesty, however large the temptation. God sees and knows our weaknesses. Escape is there before the sin is committed. He had made a way of escape. And escape is there after the sin is committed. God dwells with the contrite and humble heart and forgives. But excuses? No.

False pictures of God color the imagination of large numbers of individuals. Some see Him as a kind of super Santa Claus, concerned only that everyone should be tucked into bed at night with the assurance that at least he has had a good time. The thing about that is that the good times don't come all that often, which makes for a very weak deity. Others fabricate a Benign Indifference who lets things rock along and whose major contributions are climate, food, and sunshine.

Others want a god more like themselves. Having decided that they possess greater moral worth, better racial background, or higher education than someone else, they create a personal or national deity who agrees with their judgments. This makes it easy to imagine God taking sides against a neighbor or with one nation against another nation.

Marshall McLuhan, a Canadian communications pundit, told a group of religious broadcasters that their greatest problem was that they purveyed good news. Good news, he said, offends people. It criticizes their life-style by implication. Bad news puts us all in a position where we can elevate our egos by comparison with others' acts.

The gospel starts behind because it gives the news that degrees of wrongness don't count. The gospel proclaims changed lives, not justification by comparison.

Who wouldn't like to believe that his sin doesn't count—that it's the other fellow's that matters? Hence the offense in the sacrifice of Christ. It levels everybody down and says that all need cleansing. "There is no one who is righteous" (Romans 3:10, TEV). If you would like a God's-eye view of humanity, read Romans 3. It's guaranteed to make any ego feel uncomfortable.

Man doesn't like the way God says it is to be. Sin, forgiveness, sacrifice, cleansing, take it all out of man's control. In Eden the devil offered an alternative to enlightenment and fulfillment. Since then the philosophers and religionists of a hundred nations and cults have tried to join him in making man *feel* right but failing to *put* him right.

"Education, culture, the exercise of the will, human effort, all have their proper sphere, but here they are powerless. They may produce an outward correctness of behavior, but they cannot change the heart; they cannot purify the springs of life. There must be a power working from within, a new life from above, before men can be changed from sin to holiness. That power is Christ. His grace alone can quicken the lifeless faculties of the soul, and attract it to God, to holiness" (E. G. White, *Steps to Christ*, p. 18).

In Old Delhi we paused beside a Jain temple. A young priest came to talk about his religion. He told us that all forms of life house the potential of uniting with the infinite oneness—that nothing should be killed. He discussed the theological problems posed by the discovery of the electron microscope. Once a gauze mask sufficed to protect small life forms from ingestion and destruction. Then microscopes revealed animalcules and bacteria. A filter helped somewhat. But now the electron microscope had penetrated to the filterable and nonfilterable viruses. No longer was it enough to step high over a column of ants. One had to consider whether viruses had the same life potential as a monkey or a mouse!

What a road to holiness that projects!

Comparing ourselves with others as a way to God falsifies the path just as completely. "I am the way," Jesus pointed out, and He offered no other.

Of the salvation God gives, the Bible says, "For it is by God's grace that you have been saved, through faith. It is not your own doing, but God's gift" (Ephesians 2:8, TEV). We didn't even get in on the planning stages of the operation. Our input was neither requested nor needed. The Expert in salvation took over and devised the whole operation. Wouldn't you rather have it that way?

Humanity trips at the simplicity of God's plan—God's giving Himself to pay the penalty and to redeem. Somehow we want to share in our own salvation. We oscillate between the pitfalls of legalism and ethics—we say consciously through our creeds and philosophies and unconsciously through our deeds that there must be a better, more ego-satisfying, way. We recoil from the pain of the cross that Christ has offered to us.

Yet man never can be the captain of his own salvation. God knows and we should know that it will never work that way. Because we did not have the means to make it our own way, God came and gave us Christ. What a tragedy when we won't even try it His way!

Before we turn to the ubiquitous god kit of self-righteousness and make ourselves a god to please us, we owe it to ourselves to seek the way God tells us He does it. "Salvation is to be found through him alone; for there is no one else in all the world, whose name God has given to men, by whom we can be saved" (Acts 4:12, TEV).

Let the Sun
Shine Through

Spring had stripped the trunks of the eucalyptus trees of last year's drab bark. Now the whole forest glowed softly with strong blocks of orange and mauve where the sun caught the new bark and splashed its color against the green undergrowth of the hillside. Tall spikes of blue sun orchids hungrily tracked the setting orb. Now and again snatches of their aroma drifted through the open car window.

This was Australia's bushland at September's loveliest.

The ochers and pinks of sandstone cliffs shaded white flannelflowers roseated in their lacework of green. A profusion of wild flowers spread a palette of color on every hand. Gold banksia, cerise boronia, yellow and brown bush peas, daubed themselves across the afternoon.

Then came civilization. Neat orange groves, plowed fields, rows of juvenile cabbages. Such orderliness seemed almost obscene after the abandon of the bush. Then another corner, and a double line of color that stretched to the far bend in the road. Such a carpet of pink demanded our attention. Escaped flowers from a farm nearby? Someone's personal contribution to ecology?

From the open door of the car we looked down the road with its fringes of brilliant pink, then back the way we had come. Now the flowers had vanished. Looking ahead—they glowed against the evening sun. Looking behind, and something had wiped them out. What was it? A closer look revealed half-dead stalks of an early grass, dead brownish husks now empty of seed. And the sun! Penetrating the translucent husks, the beams of light transformed them. The dead fiber took on light and life from the brilliance of the sun's rays.

"But unto you that fear my name shall the Sun of righteousness arise with healing in his wings" (Malachi 4:2, KJV).

Can the Sun transform the spent?

Let's call him Joe.

Two thousand people had packed a theater to hear the preacher. Every type of humanity paraded through the lobby. Staff members bustled among them, greeting regulars, welcoming strangers.

Joe entered as the choir began the theme song.

He was dirty. Not with the grime that comes from the shop or the farm but with unwashed dirt that accumulates over weeks of soapless drought. He shuffled by with averted eyes and a drifting reek of tobacco and sweat. An alert usher slipped ahead of him and diverted him to an empty section of the theater, then sat sentry at the end of the row.

Watching from the rear, we noted Joe's interest and wondered.

Next morning the evangelist distributed names to his staff. There was Joe's—no doubt about it, for who else would give his address as the city trash dump?

It became a matter of weekly interest to hear the reports on Joe. He came regularly to meetings. At first there was no difference in grime or dress. Then his face grew a little whiter, the grubbiness slowly eroded.

On his first visit the team member had found Joe raking over loads of trash. Stacks of bottles, heaps of aluminum and copper, piles of household rejects of doubtful salability, indicated his livelihood. Joe had built himself a shelter of old pieces of iron and wood. Inside smelled the same as outside, but the pastor entered and prayed with Joe.

Then came the day when the pastor helped Joe get ready for his first Sabbath service. For a week the fuss went on—a new apartment, clean clothes, looking for a job, prayer about tobacco and alcohol, finally the big cleanup with a scrub brush in a tub of hot water.

Achievement and uncertainty jostled inside Joe as he stepped down the aisle of the church clutching hymnbook and Bible. He had come a long way. I remember him that day—hair trimmed, face shaven, as self-conscious as a boy on his first date. I remember the tears on baptism day.

Every so often I go by the church where Joe now serves as head deacon. "Remember?" he says. "Remember?"

Thank You, Sun of righteousness.

And I say to myself, "Find another shell, Lord, let the Sun shine through."

"God's mercy is so abundant, and his love for us so great, that while we were spiritually dead in our disobedience he brought us to life in Christ. It is by God's grace that you have been saved" (Ephesians 2:4, 5, TEV).

Consider Ralph de Jesus—twelve years old, hooked on heroin. He testifies before a presidential commission on drugs, telling of the social pressures. The ten-year-old boy who couldn't say no to cigarettes or marijuana. The eleven-year-old who joined a gang to rob and threaten for the money to support a drug habit. The twelve-year-old who found Jesus, his Namesake, and found a way out. The twelve-year-old who startles the commission with a ringing testimony to the power of Christ.

For us all it could be good-bye to that Doctor Jekyll and Mr. Hyde existence. Our secret lives could match our public lives. The mockery of hypocrisy could transform in the presence of the Transformer. It isn't our doing. God tells us it's His.

Every husk awaits the Sun of righteousness. Every facade hides the human who might be the reflection of deity.

This is what Jesus meant when He proclaimed, "I am the light of the world." John confirms this: "The Word was the source of life, and this life brought light to men. The light shines in the darkness, and the darkness has never put it out" (John 1:4, 5, TEV).

What changed the husks of grass to their beauty? Fellowship with the sun. And fellowship with the Sun can change your life. "If, then, we say that we have fellowship with him, yet at the same time live in the darkness, we are lying both in our words and in our actions. But if we live in the light—just as he is in the light—then we have fellowship with one another, and the blood of Jesus, his Son, makes us clean from every sin" (1 John 1:6, 7, TEV).

Who needs the fellowship of the Son?

He came with the price of education and wealth on his shoulders. He had never read how hard the path goes for the rich. He had not yet considered the Biblical needle nor judged how the eye would scrape at his wealth and education before he passed through to the kingdom. But he came.

Need brought him. He had tried everything that education could suggest or money could buy. Then he remembered Christianity—not the formal sort to which he'd already conformed, but the kind a friend had told him about, the kind that changes and gives direction to life.

For a while it seemed that he would replay the story of the rich young ruler, for he had great riches. But he had been that route, and now the need pressed in, and the Son said come.

And God neither impoverished him nor made him a nincompoop, but He did change him. If you are ready for change, God is ready for you. That's what Christianity is all about—change. Change for the better, change to a new life.

"To those who, like the young ruler, are in high positions of trust and have great possessions, it may seem too great a sacrifice to give up all in order to follow Christ. But this is the rule of conduct for all who would become His disciples. Nothing short of obedience can be accepted" (E. G. White, *The Desire of Ages*, p. 523).

No one can cloak himself with self and let the Sun shine through. Unless a man is changed, converted, he cannot enter the kingdom of heaven.

To many God seems impertinent because He

changes and asks for change. Couldn't He leave us alone and still look after us and bring us to eternal life? Just a little help would be enough. Just enough change to get us through this crisis. I have the feeling that if there were any other way for God to accomplish man's happiness, He would have done it that way. The sacrifice of Calvary shows the measure of man's plight. That it should take such a price reveals the desperate situation into which sin has placed us. That God's good Son would leave heaven, suffer, and die tells us something of the abject need of every human heart.

In Christ a universal need meets the Universal Solution. Race, creed, condition, hold no barriers to the advance of God's love. "Your world was a world without hope and without God. But now in union with Christ Jesus you who once were far off have been brought near through the shedding of Christ's blood. For he is himself our peace" (Ephesians 2:12-14, NEB).

Christianity schedules no tryouts. It's all right to urge, "Try it; you'll like it." Christianity can stand that kind of approach. But no one can discover it on a part-time basis. Flirting at the edges of Christ's teachings may give high ethics, fine morals. It may generate goodwill, and good manners; but to create change, surrender must come. No arguments, no ifs, no buts, no conditions—simply surrender.

It appears elsewhere in this book, but let me say here that surrender isn't obliteration of personality or individuality. Christianity isn't a negative or an absence. It's a positive and a Presence. No one ever really knows himself for what he might be and should be until he knows Christ.

Directions

Remember, too, that God's point of departure is where you stand now. Who comes to Christ must make no journey to a landing strip before he takes off on his flight to eternal life. He climbs no steps to reach the launching pad. He builds no bridge to close the gap between himself and righteousness. The flight starts where you are. The launch begins where you stand, with God bridging in to your side of the gap.

How do you evaluate yourself spiritually? An empty stalk by the roadside of life? a dead husk? No matter.

The Sun of righteousness still shines!

So You'd Like to Know Your Future?

A recent full-page ad in many American dailies reminded that during World War II more than one statesman headed to his local astrologer to determine the national course of action. We'd like to think things have changed, but the "future" business never had it as good as it does today. It doesn't seem right that, despite education, sophistication, and cynicism, more and more people consult horoscopes, revel in the predictions of phony prophets, and join séances. But that's the way it is.

Certainly Nebuchadnezzar would have no trouble assembling his coterie of wise men from the columnists, television personalities, and authors who engage in the fascinating game of crystal gazing.

It pays to step back and see how well the better of them do. Here's a look at the failures of Maurice Woodruff, an English clairvoyant who enjoyed remarkable television audiences. Back in 1967 he predicted as follows:

The Vietnam war would end in May, 1967—it ended in April, 1975.

General de Gaulle would be put out of office during 1967—he chose to quit his office April 28, 1969.

The Americans would beat the Russians in placing a man on the moon by a matter of hours, late in 1969 or early 1970. The Americans made it July 20, 1969, but the Russians haven't made it yet.

Second-guessing himself in early 1969 he prophesied the end of the Vietnam conflict in April of that year. It wasn't till March 29, 1973, that the last U.S. Air Force contingent left Vietnam.

Then, of course, there was that band of clearvisioned seers who expected a major portion of California to slip, Atlantislike, under the Pacific Ocean in the month of April, 1969.

And don't forget the Children of God who filled the streets of America with leaflets predicting the end of the world with the arrival of the comet Kohoutek, January 5, 1974.

"More than ten thousand fashionable seers, stargazers, and assorted swamis now make their living —and often a very good living—telling Americans about their future and how to face it. From the pulpit of television their pontifications are soaked up as gospel truth. Enlightened leaders in politics and finance, stars of stage and screen, base crucial decisions on their favorite astrologer's glorified guesswork" (Leslie Lieber, "Can Anyone Predict the Future?" *This Week* [Supplement to the Washington *Star*], November 2, 1969).

Despite all the zeros on the scoreboards of prediction, they keep coming back with more guesses. Imagination, an ability for oracular sayings, and a little gimmickry stoke the boilers of baloney, and people line up to buy the product. In recent years several astrologers have even programmed computers to handle the conjunction of planets and constellations.

You can imagine how Jeane Dixon felt October 20, 1968, when she saw the morning paper. Her column for the day predicted: "I will stand on my New Year's prediction and see no marriage for Jackie [Kennedy] in the near future." Trying to rescue disaster, she used the time lag between Europe and America in a frantic attempt to recall the column. But in many papers it appeared along with the announcement of Jackie's marriage to Aristotle Onassis.

Actually it's only a little more difficult to count up successes than to tot up the failures. It's just that the successes get the publicity. Jeane Dixon's average isn't that wonderful; she has good press agents. Most of us have forgotten her memorable guess that war would break out between the United States and China in 1958 and the other one that Red China would join the UN in 1959, something that didn't occur until October, 1971.

Yet people love their prophets. Ruth Montgomery tells in Jeane Dixon's life story, *A Gift of Prophecy,* of a vision shortly after midnight July 14, 1952. Jeane Dixon claims that a great snake came to her room and enfolded her body. Watching without apparent fear, she saw the head of the serpent turn eastward. Taking this as an omen, she began to look to the East for guidance.

Adding to the mystery, she proclaimed the birth of a child on February 5, 1962, in the Middle East who would revolutionize the world. This child will bring a new Christianity to the world and will answer the prayers of all mankind!

Eileen J. Garrett, a medium and president of the

American Society for Psychical Research, attacked the "shabby trade of the soothsayer" in her book *The Sense and Nonsense of Prophecy*. Americans, she wrote, sneer at anything they cannot see or understand, but they flock in droves to spend huge sums of money on such astounding revelations as: "You're a good friend but a dangerous enemy" or "Don't argue with the boss next Wednesday."

Even Christian journals cannot keep their fingers out of the astrology pie. In a recent issue of *Church World*, the weekly Catholic newspaper published in Maine, Annette Bousquet Jones used the signs of the zodiac for a series of spiritual meditations.

"What will the future do to me?" seems like a very reasonable question to ask. It isn't a new question. The Latins slew animals and studied the layout of their entrails to determine the course a battle should take. They also studied storms, winds, and comets. The Greeks gave us the word *oracular* from the popular priests of Delphi who mouthed obscure, double-entendre prophecies.

The Bible lumps all these human guessings together as part of a great trick to keep us from the source of true knowledge. They are part of the lying signs and wonders that deceive the world—and we are to expect that they will grow more common in the last days. One of the gravest dangers is that they will direct us away from the prophecy of the Bible.

"So we are even more confident of the message proclaimed by the prophets. You will do well to pay attention to it, because it is like a lamp shining in a dark place, until the Day dawns and light of the morning star shines in your hearts" (2 Peter 1:19, TEV).

An open mind can soon discover the accuracy

of Bible prophecies; there are enough of them to test. A simple exercise in history will match the gold, silver, brass, iron, iron and clay of Nebuchadnezzar's image in Daniel 2 with the empires of Babylon, Medo-Persia, Greece, Rome, and a divided western Europe.

Again, take a pen and write down the prophecies of Christ the Messiah in the Old Testament and check them against the record of His life. The list will include the place of birth, time of death, price of betrayal, manner of death, and on and on. Another exercise might include a comparison between the history of ancient cities of the eastern Mediterranean coast and the predictions of the Scripture.

If the Bible has so much to say about the past and one can adduce evidence of the accuracy of the prophecies contained in the Holy Writ, why chase after the modern soothsayer? Why not see if the Bible has anything to say about the future? Perhaps it's because most people don't see the Bible as a book about the future; they regard it as a book about the ancient wisdom of the past. Perhaps it's because astrological predictions are less probing or demanding than those of the Bible. Perhaps it's because the Bible conditions its pleasanter prophecies on a changed life.

Yet for identity and destiny one can't approach a surer source than the Bible. If insecurity and uncertainty are driving a generation back to the Ouija board, it is only because people are ignorant of or have failed to find out about the security and certainty the Bible offers, not just for the future of the race, but also for personal fates.

Take a look at what the Bible says about people. It says man once was perfect, a son of God. Now that status is gone, usurped by an evil power called

Satan. In his fallen state man is depraved, dissolute, lost. He isn't climbing the ladder of evolutionary progression to galactic stardom; he's going down to certain oblivion. But the lost status can be restored through Jesus Christ. That's the surprising, good thing about Jesus Christ: He gives us back our sonship.

On this rock of identity God builds the future for His people. He can and will control events to design a future free from uncertainty and insecurity.

The pattern of the future isn't beautiful in some aspects. Political unity will escape the best endeavors of the race (Daniel 2). While summitry tries its hand to solve the financial headaches of the world, conflict between worker and employer will continue (James 5). Streets will be infested with thugs and muggers, and the locks of our doors will be of little value (Matthew 24). If you're worried about the mounting population and the threat of mass hunger, no comfort comes from Jesus' predictions of conditions before His coming (Matthew 24).

Pollution will foul the environment of mankind far into the future until God singles it out for special attention in the end of time (Revelation 11:18 and 16:3, 4). Tension and stress, major health hazards of the late twentieth century, aren't going to disappear down the tranquilizer bottle (Luke 21:25, 26). Nor will the worst of tensions—that between races and nations—grow less (Daniel 2; Matthew 24:6, 7).

On the brighter side we should not expect any slackening in the technological revolution that has given us satellites and other communications marvels—God plans to use them to finish His work (Daniel 12:4). Christianity will not subside before the onslaughts of skepticism, Eastern religions, and indifference—it is destined to reach every creature (Matthew 24:14). Despite all the catastrophes of the last days, God will develop and preserve a faithful people who will share His new world with Him (Revelation 14:1-5, 12).

Lest you think there is something mystic or marvelous about divine predictions, let's turn it toward individuals. While the Bible doesn't give horoscopes, it gives an accurate portrayal of the fates awaiting every person. Though the way each person takes to find himself at his ultimate destiny may not be revealed, that destiny is never in doubt. "Then the king will say to those on his right hand, 'You have my Father's blessing; come, enter and possess the kingdom that has been ready for you since the world was made.' . . . Then he will say to those on his left hand, 'The curse is upon you; go from my sight to the eternal fire that is ready for the devil and his angels.' . . . And they will go away to eternal punishment, but the righteous will enter eternal life" (Matthew 25: 34-46, NEB).

How does one come to these conditions?

Here is Jesus' explanation: " 'Go in through the narrow gate, because the gate is wide and the road is easy that leads to hell, and there are many who travel it. The gate is narrow and the way is hard that leads to life, and few people find it' " (Matthew 7:13, 14, TEV).

Two roads—one to life, one to death. And the Lord suggests that it isn't easy to find the way to life. God's destiny isn't so much hidden from view as it is unacceptable. It requires certain admissions, surrender to another power, and dependency on that power for the rest of your life. To many, "Eat, drink, and be merry" attracts far more. Worse yet, the devil's nudge always pushes away from God. Counteracting that pressure keeps every Christian on the alert.

Yet a frank appraisal of one's future on the broad way should give one pause. The first few steps that take one past pleasure, money, education, seem innocent enough. One could find the same waymarks on the narrow path. But soon these become ends rather than means, and the way broadens, accommodating greed, pride, and license. Yes, there's faith on the broad way, faith in oneself, the system, the corporation, the bank account. And even these are not all that wrong, except that they blind one to faith in God.

But it isn't long before the thoughtful traveler finds the emptiness of a God-bereft life. He may not diagnose it as that at once. A feeling of dissatisfaction with life, of thwarted development, of purposelessness, of disillusionment, grips the life. He walks the wrong way and knows it but does not know why. Such a person may decide that means really are ends and chase money or power. More tragically, he may opt for alcohol, drugs, or suicide to satisfy the "dis-ease."

God doesn't gild the destination of this road. His new world could not absorb the greed, hate, lust, fear, anger, that ride with the walkers on the broad way.

One doesn't have to go too far into the Bible to predict the fate of many people in the world. The trouble is that the prediction isn't popular and isn't believed.

Many would accept the alternative if it didn't ask so much of them. Who wouldn't decide for eternal life, freedom from guilt, a meaning and purpose to life, and other rewards almost without end? It doesn't take much to sell the goals of Christianity. Many people want the goals without the methodology. They want to be there, but they don't want to walk the narrow road. Trust is okay, but obey? Heaven, yes, for sure, but commandments? Freedom from guilt, yes, but accept Christ?

Like to know your future with God? The Bible gives the final destination; the way between will depend on God and you.

David couldn't see beyond the sheep and his harp until God sent him to fight Goliath and put him on the road to the throne.

Judas figured he had the system licked until his trickery turned against him and condemned him as traitor of the Best Man who ever lived.

Peter thought he had lost his chance to show his love for Christ when the cock crowed, but Jesus designed a new future for him and told him to "feed my sheep."

A contrast between the lives on the broad way and the lives on the narrow way develops as we look back into history. The Bible shows what might be ours.

David looked into the future, saw it as a projection of his past with God, and wrote the Shepherd's Psalm to celebrate. Had the psalmist been a modern, might he have written like this?

"The Lord is my consultant; my future is secure.

"He gives me peace of mind. He helps me relax and eases away stress and tension.

"He builds up my confidence: He leads me to consistency and inner oneness so that I praise His goodness.

"Even though I feel threatened with cancer, or automobile accidents, or heart disease, or crime, I will not panic or fear. You stay at my side. Your counsel guides me day and night.

"Despite the omens of destruction and an environment in jeopardy, I know You hold the future in Your hands. Even inflation doesn't leave me insecure.

"Surely goodness and mercy shall follow me all the days of my life: and I will dwell in the house of the Lord for ever."

Can anyone predict the future? Indeed, yes. You and I can even choose the future we will have.

It's the
Real Thing

Above the throb and bustle of the bazaars that line the north entrance to the Temple of a Thousand Pillars in Madurai, India, rose the rat-a-tat-tat of a drum. Pressing through the festival crowd I found a circle of onlookers enclosing a man and a woman.

The woman beat the rhythm of the drum. In the center of the circle stood the man, naked to the waist. A long whip snaked from his hand. The drum spoke a new command, his face tightened, the thong snarled out and lashed around his body. Blood flowed as the lashes at the end of the whip chopped at his side and arm.

A few months before I had stood in the great cobblestone plaza of the shrine of Guadalupe in Mexico City. A gold rose, blessed by the pope, would be enshrined near the altar on the morrow. Pilgrims thronged the plaza honoring the anniversary of the day when a peasant reported his vision of the virgin Mary some four hundred years before.

Near the center of the square a farmer struggled forward on his knees toward the distant entrance to the shrine. Every few yards he rested, stained hands raised in prayer. His children walked with him, lending their thin shoulders as support or spreading rags to pad his knees from the coarse cobbles.

Inside the shrine our guide pushed his way toward the tattered piece of cloth that the devout believe bears a photolike impression of the vision. It was received on the peasant's cloak as the vision burned its way earthward. Each time a gap opened in the throng there would be someone on his knees torturing himself toward the plaque with its ancient piece of rag.

The real thing?

Well, it's all done in the name of God or god. And isn't God love? And isn't love the real thing?

The Indian whipping his body does it in the name of god. The peasant inching across the plaza does it for his God. In their own way they are crying out, "Notice me. See what I am doing for you. See what I suffer. Now repay me with kindness and blessing."

The idea of stern justice demanding retribution or appeasement developed long ago in the history of mankind. The Israelites copied it during their more degenerate apostasies from neighboring Canaanite tribes. The early Christian church caught the contagion of penance from the pagan cults and purification rites of the various religions in the Roman Empire. But these are not Christianity. The only time a man tried to buy salvation in the apostles' times, he was rebuked, and his name became the byword for seeking influence and spiritual power by illegitimate methods. We still call it simony.

Christianity approaches the dilemma of depravity from another angle: "God loved the world so much that he gave his only Son, so that everyone who believes in him may not die but have eternal life" (John 3:16, TEV).

The operative word is *love*. Now, *love* has taken on a lot of baggage through the years, and it means many things. But a little study will unearth the real thing.

A little of the compelling power of the love Christ generated in the hearts of His disciples may be sensed in the explosion of conversion that began at Pentecost. Tacitus, a contemporary of Paul and a reasonably able historian, records, "Christus, the founder of the name [Christian], had undergone the death penalty in the reign of Tiberius, by the sentence of the procurator Pontius Pilatus, and the pernicious superstition was checked for a moment."

Yet by the year AD 64, when he was putting down the events of that era, he spoke of the followers of Jesus as "vast numbers."

Kirby Page speaks of the unbelievable miracle of Christianity this way: "If it had not actually happened it would be regarded as absolutely impossible. That the religion of an obscure teacher in a conquered province, who himself was crucified as a common malefactor, should spread within three centuries, in spite of vigorous opposition and bitter persecution, so rapidly that it became the official religion of the mightiest empire of all the earth: this is simply incredible" (*Jesus or Christianity*, p. 53).

The difference between Christianity and the established religions of the day lay in the concept that God loves. When John wrote, "God is love," he was saying something that had never really been thought of seriously before. Gods might be many different things—immoral, sensuous, vindictive, dishonest, tricky, stern, fierce, cruel, vicious—but for God to be love staggered the thinking of that day and set in train concepts that still have validity and freshness today.

"The influence of His life, His words, and His death, have, from the first, been like leaven cast into the mass of humanity. He made religion spiritual instead of ceremonial and external; universal, instead of local. He gave us the magnificent dowry of a faith in One Common Father of the whole human race, and, thus, of a world-wide brotherhood of all mankind. . . . All that love to our fellowman can prompt finds itself only a copy of that life which was spent in continually doing good, and the noblest self-sacrifice for others finds itself anticipated by Calvary" (Cunningham Geikie, *The Life and Words of Christ*, pp. vii, viii).

Herein lies hope. If God is love, then meaning enters life. We are here because of love, because God wanted us and made us. We may hope that the same love will set things right for us.

Love gives hope. "Such a hope is no mockery, because God's love has flooded our inmost heart through the Holy Spirit he has given us. For at the very time when we were still powerless, then Christ died for the wicked" (Romans 5:5, 6, NEB).

What does it mean for God to love? How does this love help?

Do you remember the geometry of the circle? A constant factor holds the key to understanding the circle. Only as you insert the constant π into the equations about the circle can you resolve them.

God's love enters the equations of life as the constant that makes sense of them. Try to understand life without the presence of God's love, and bitterness and disillusion follow.

Life in the twentieth century poses more than its share of problems. Young and old are afflicted with them. Suicide ranks as the No. 2 killer of college-age people, claiming in 1971 3,620 lives of youth under the age of twenty-five. If only these people could have let the constant of God's love into the puzzling equations that forced them to take their own lives, they would not have become statistics.

God's love starts from His side toward our side. "We love him, because he first loved us." Such a love has no need of qualifications, nor does it ask for them, because it has already decided on the price that must be paid, has given considered thought to the nature of those to be helped, and has decided to go ahead anyway. God initiated love toward us. We didn't have to do penance or flagellate our bodies to earn that love; all we had to do was to be human.

Nothing can reduce, destroy, modify, or deflect the love of God in Christ. Like the air we breathe, it is always there. Before we knew Him as a God of love, He was loving us; if we cease to see Him that way, He will never stop loving us just the same. No matter how we object to the insertion of the factor of love into our lives, it asserts its own trajectory to match our every move.

By our actions and words we continually try

to obligate others to us. Bribery springs from such self-seeking motivation, and so do a host of other things—some good, some bad. Sin was born out of a desire to satisfy self. We do it to each other all the time by seeking to obligate others and so build up self. Cain tried it on God with the produce of his own originating, the mistake that all of us make at one time or another. He thought God was like him and could be obligated by a good turn, a gift, or a deed done in His favor.

It would only be sad if it were not also dangerous. Some people actually believe they can get God on their side by what they do. God's answer to this is: "It is by his grace you are saved, through trusting him; it is not your own doing. It is God's gift, not a reward for work done" (Ephesians 2:8, 9, NEB).

Sometimes the quality or quantity of our involvement in sin worries us. We are so bad or what we have done is so evil that we think ourselves beyond the pale of mercy. God says no. "God has shown us how much he loves us; it was while we were still sinners that Christ died for us!" (Romans 5:8, TEV).

God did not wait to begin the venture of salvation until a group of people had proved their worth; He sent His Son to die for the unworthy. Even doing battle against God and His love does not exclude us. One may fight God and still receive His love. "We were God's enemies, but he made us his friends through the death of his Son" (Romans 5:10, TEV).

God's love has behind it all the authority and power of omnipotence. Nothing can hinder the release of its power within the life that accepts it.

It operates toward all men, but it operates best and most powerfully in the life that delights in its influence.

In the days when go-karts filled the brown eyes of my son with visions of exciting races and hair-raising speeds, I conceived a plan and made it a promise. I would take an old motor mower, strip the engine from the chassis, and fashion a go-kart. For weeks he asked, "When?" while I pondered, "How?" Finally came confession day, and I had to admit that I could not fulfill that promise. Even my love and my desire could not produce within me the skills I needed to do what I had pledged.

Best of all the things about God's love is His ability to keep His promises. "O fear the Lord, ye his saints: for there is no want to them that fear him. . . . They that seek the Lord shall not want any good thing" (Psalm 34:9, 10, KJV).

May I introduce you to the mystery of the moment when we discover God's love and let it loose in our lives? "See how much the Father has loved us! His love is so great that we are called God's children—and so, in fact, we are" (1 John 3:1, TEV).

Remember, God's love asks nothing of us but surrender and acceptance. He assigns no goals to attain, no preparation to make, before He welcomes us. We have the only qualification we need: we are human, and Christ died to seek and to save this lost race.

Christ has been looking in love at you and me from the moment of our births. He won't stop that loving. He waits for us to accept it. That's the real thing that makes the difference to living: "God is love."

Shore Break

There is a moment when the wave is kind and you are alone with the onrushing, downcurving water that riding the surf seems the only thing in the wide world worth doing.

Whether you mount a board or pit muscle and flesh against the rolling drive of a breaker, exhilaration floods as tons of water propel you onward through the shore break.

Nothing provides quite the physical satisfaction as when crashing down the front of a ten-foot wall of water curling with the power of a distant storm. For a few seconds you live in the midst of a battle between the raging power of the wave in its shoreward rush and the outward pull of water building for the next wave.

Thousands adopt this as their passion each year.

Yet many times when I have tried to introduce friends to the mystique of the wave, they have lacked the balance, judgment, and touch of daring that makes it possible to ride a wave.

Judgment is the key. In an instant one must decide whether the shape, height, position, and curl of the wave approve commitment to its power.

Sometimes bodysurfing, I have ridden with the wave, only to look down and see just a very few inches of water between the base of the breaker and the sandy bottom. *That* wave one lets go by.

Errors in judgment teach that water packs a mighty punch. It can pick you up, roll you over, tumble you as if you were in a washing machine, slap you hard on the ocean bottom, and finally grate you like a giant carrot across the sand while all the time your body shrieks for air.

Once while riding a wave, I caught a glimpse of the sandy floor seven or eight feet below and decided to wait for another curler. A surfing acquaintance judged the wave differently. He committed himself. I caught a view of him struggling through the shore break, face distorted in pain, arm hanging broken and limp at his side.

Only in the shore break do you really know what success the venture in the water has been.

But this is not a treatise on how to ride the wild surf!

Except that . . .

Judgment, decision, and a little daring are the very ingredients of life. Rightly developed, they provide the touchstone to success.

We say, "He rode to success on a wave of popularity," as if he had nothing to do with it—as if chance brought the rewards and swept him holus-bolus to unanticipated fame.

Does it ever really happen that way?

For several years a seesaw battle had raged along the North African coast between the British, Australians, Indians, and New Zealanders on one hand and Germans and Italians on the other. Rommel, it seemed, would gain the ultimate victory for the Germans.

From the ranks of Allied generals the leaders chose a fiery little man called Montgomery. Impatient superiors urged him to launch his counter-offensive. But Monty took his time. Fighting a holding action, he spent weeks building resources and stockpiles of material. Finally the moment arrived. The push began, ending with the surrender of the Axis forces in that part of the world and the conquest of North Africa.

Experience gave the moment for striking.

Listen to this: "But when the right time finally came, God sent his own Son" (Galatians 4:4, TEV).

Think of the conjunction of events necessary for God to choose the moment for Jesus' entry into the world! Not just the right descendant of David and at the right time, but the condition of Judea, its rulers, its people, access to potential disciples, the strength of pagan religions, the power of Judaism. These, plus uncounted other factors, had to be programmed into the decision to ensure the success of Christ's mission.

And remember, the basic decisions had to be made no less than five hundred years before the action began. God gave Daniel accurate information about the timing of Christ's appearance, and there could be no turning back from that moment on.

God had no certain control over the diodes and circuits of the computer of history. He could see ahead, yes. But each of the thousands who played a part, finally bringing "the right time," acted independently, capriciously, humanly.

Thus God judged and used the wave of history to bring us salvation.

What a God!

What a risk that the shore break would find us floundering without help! But He did it. What daring! What judgment! What love!

But we can't be omniscient, all-wise, like God. Life demands decisions, asks judgments, and often provides no basis for making them. *Time* looked at a group of successful young men a few years back and tried to analyze the factors that led to their rise. *Time* opted for judgment in decision as the prime factor. "On balance, the people who are paid best are those who are regularly called upon to display one of the most valuable of all commodities: judgment" (*Time*, February 28, 1969).

The main problem with spiritual judgments as opposed to secular ones lies in the matter of control. One has far more control over which stocks will provide the best security than over his temper. And it's easier to choose a tie than to choose not to smoke, as millions of would-be quitters have discovered.

In secular judgments the wise look at all sides of the question, consider the possible outcome of each of several decisions, and then choose. Leaders rise and fall on the quality of their decisions. Our lives show happiness or failure on the quality of the choices we make.

Spiritually the choices can be without thought of consequence, as was Eve's decision to pluck the fruit. It came from the pressure and temptation of the moment. Availability and desirability are hard forces to resist.

Directions

Decision may come also in the face of popular opinion. Thor Heyerdahl rode a raft across the Pacific because he judged differently from most men. Noah took up the ax to fell the first gopher tree and begin the framework of the ark because he judged God believable, despite the sneers of the experts.

Sometimes serendipity springs surprises. Sometimes disaster wipes out expectations. But for most of our lives our decisions will make us what we are.

Early in life we begin to form patterns of decisions. Friends are not forced on us; we choose them. Health habits ultimately become more than a parent's nagging; they become choice. Sooner or later one has to answer the question "What are you going to be when you grow up?" Standards of behavior, style of dress, modes of thought and speech—all these lie within the power of decision. What we need is the happy knack of choosing the smart way to go.

It's much easier to quarterback your life from the perspective of the morning after. Here is Peter weeping bitterly after his denial of the Saviour, here is Judas tightening the noose around his own neck, here is King Saul confessing his foolishness in not destroying the Amalekites completely, here is Solomon in old age pontificating on the dangers of dalliance. We get "too soon old and too late smart."

Consider Peter, curious, heartbroken, but determined to witness the trial of his Master, slipping through the back entrance to the palace of the high priest. While Jesus faced the council, Peter sat with the servants, catching the latest news of the trial from them.

A teenage girl spotted him. "I know you. You were with Jesus." Peter shrank from some of the alternates he saw down the road—exposure, possible trial. A wave began to build. Peter opted for lies, rationalizing that it was surely better to live and try to help Jesus after the trial than be thrust front and center alongside the Saviour.

Another servant spotted him. Perhaps the first had whispered her suspicions around the fireplace. "That man there was with Jesus!" she accused. Peter shriveled. What if the man whose ear he had sliced off appeared? The wave rises higher.

In the final scene Peter convinces his accusers by swearing. No one would suspect him of belonging with Jesus after that outburst. Then, just as the wave seemed to be carrying safely, the rooster crowed backstage. Jesus looked at him. Remorse buried him. If only . . .

All through that bitter day, past the cross and the resurrection, Peter floundered for his footing. Even Jesus' personal message, "Go and tell Peter," did not put him on his feet.

Yet his failure was not beyond retrieval. No human failure lies beyond hope in the spiritual world until probation closes.

Despite the resurrection and the miracles of Jesus' appearance, the disciples possessed no clear vision of the path they should choose. Nothing in the three and a half years with Jesus had prepared them for this sudden separation. Looking into a bleak and hopeless future without the Man they loved, they judged life not only empty but even dangerous if their enemies found them out.

Peter turned the clock back: "I'm going fishing."

They joined him at the old familiar trade. They had fished for men for three years. It had been exciting work. But that was over. Now back to what they knew best how to do.

They caught no fish. Did they remember that other night when they had come empty-handed to a gray morning? Jesus didn't forget. He stood on the shore and called to them, "Have you caught anything?"

Not one of them expected Jesus on that morning of discouragement. He was a stranger shouting from the shore, "Put down your nets on the other side of the boat."

Peter's reflexes bogged in remorse. But John remembered. "It is the Lord!" he shouted.

Peter jumped over the side of the boat and headed for shore. The others kept hauling in the fish. They did not know that they would not need those fish. Jesus had breakfast ready for them. He had answered their need before they recognized it.

But the miracle draft had its own message. Once He had called them this way. Now He told them things hadn't changed. Men still needed their ministry. The mission He had come to commence would now continue through them.

And for Peter there was the moment of reinstatement. The commission: "Feed my sheep"; the question: "Lovest thou me?"

Peter didn't know that he had already set in motion Christ's concern and love the moment he had left those nets years before. From that day on he was Christ's man moving in a different sphere, cared for in a way he could not know. His decision to follow Christ brought the wisdom and judgment of heaven onto his side. As long as he followed Jesus there would be a way on into the future from all the choices of his life. And that way would lead him always toward God and toward eternal life. With Christ the waves of life would never leave him without the assurance of ultimate success.

Glad Song
to God

He came puttering to my side in a motorized wheelchair, Pastor Jose de Sa, director at lonely Quicuco Mission in southern Angola. Nothing about his face with its smiles of welcome, suggested the tragedy of twelve years before. A downward glance revealed the shrunken limbs, the paralyzed lower body that had kept him captive to the mechanical contrivance through all those years.

Even how it happened does not offer the not-my-fault solace of a drunken driver mishap. Such a good man should have escaped this burden.

Jose de Sa arrived in Angola during World War II to create a mission station on the site of a property bought ten years before. Lions and leopards ruled the hills and raided the plains. Local residents, tribespeople for the most part, retreated before the marauders, fearing to raise cattle and sometimes fleeing for their lives. Hyenas prowled the villages. Crops suffered from elephants and other raiders.

The villagers say of Jose that he "healed the land." With rifle and stout heart he won reprieve from the predators and defended the crops. As crops of sorghum and maize flourished the mission attracted the people.

Soon school buildings offered the first education many of these children had ever been given. The farms took on new aspects. Corn ran in rows between the baobab trees. Orchards of tropical fruits thrived. Lacking the glamour or fluency in English that other missionaries commanded, Jose de Sa built slowly, often with his own hands. Many times he envied the large gifts showered on other mission directors after visits to the United States. But the work went well.

He was laying block for the boys' dormitory when the scaffold tore loose from its support and tumbled him fifteen feet to the ground. If there had been a hospital or even a doctor close by, he might have walked again. But the trek to the medical facilities in distant Quilengues was long, and he has never walked since.

Give up? Go back to a life of ease in Portugal? He admits he thought wistfully of the sunny porch in Lisbon, where life would be easier. Then he thought of the prison it would put him in. How could he negotiate the curbs and hills of Portugal's capital? So he stayed.

A widening of the paths here, a stouter bridge there, a special wheelchair to withstand bumps and gullies, a motor to drive the chair, and he took over again. With scarcely a lost step the work of the mission marched forward again with new buildings, better education, larger appropriations. A new church, the largest Adventist church structure in Angola, graces the campus. The people look with pride and hope to the future because of their pastor, and they lift their glad song to God.

"I will lift up my voice to extol the Lord, and before a great company I will praise him" (Psalm 109:30, NEB).

"Happy is the man who fears the Lord and finds great joy in his commandments." "Bad news shall have no terrors for him, because his heart is steadfast, trusting in the Lord. His confidence is strongly based, he will have no fear" (Psalm 112:1, 7, 8, NEB).

People peppered Christ with the "why" kind of questions: the kind of questions we would ask about a man like Jose de Sa, or any other innocent one forced into suffering. Some asked Him questions to excuse their sins. Others poked an accusatory finger at their enemy or neighbor. Jesus gave comfort to neither.

"At that very time there were some people present who told him about the Galileans whose blood Pilate had mixed with their sacrifices. He answered them: 'Do you imagine that, because these Galileans suffered this fate, they must have been greater sinners than anyone else in Galilee? I tell you they were not; but unless you repent, you will all of you come to the same end' " (Luke 13:1-3, NEB).

What kind of an answer is that? Is repentance the key to escape from the consequences of an act? And what of the fact that these people were doing God's business when the government descended and slaughtered them without trial? How does what Christ said answer the problem of human suffering?

The people of Christ's day showed all the human traits that make us people. They had it all figured out. Those Galileans got themselves wiped out because of their own foolishness. In some way not particularly clear they must be less human, less good, more guilty, than those who escaped that fate. Pride pushes people to strange conclusions. Those people actually felt more righteous because someone else had suffered and they had escaped. Therefore, they concluded, God must love them more than the dead Galileans.

Jesus told them that there was something different about their death that made it applicable to the unrepentant. But it couldn't have been the injustice of the event.

" 'Or the eighteen people who were killed when the tower fell on them in Siloam—do you imagine they were more guilty than all the other people living in Jerusalem? I tell you they were not; but unless you repent, you will all of you come to the same end' " (verses 4, 5).

Those people felt relief that God had singled the eighteen out, and though they walked that way often, they had escaped. Which is another way of saying that God pushed the tower down to punish the eighteen for their wicked ways!

Was it the capriciousness of their death that made it applicable to the unrepentant?

Injustice and caprice tandem through every life.

Christ explained it all in the parable that followed. " 'A man had a fig-tree growing in his vineyard: and he came looking for fruit on it, but found none. So he said to the vinedresser, "Look here! For the last three years I have come looking for fruit on this fig-tree without finding any. Cut it down. Why should it go on using up the soil?"

But he replied, "Leave it, sir, this one year while I dig round it and manure it. And if it bears next season, well and good; if not, you shall have it down" ' " (verses 6-9).

Christ was insisting that tragedy doesn't lie in injustice or caprice—they are the common lot of humanity—tragedy comes even when suffering bears no fruit. To die at Pilate's hand or expire beneath a tumble of bricks has no purpose outside of Christ. The unrepentant have no hope, no meaning, to their death. Only in Christ does the injustice and uncertainty of life develop meaning.

In a way it's a strange answer. One might expect better of God for those who repent. Yet the Lord didn't exclude sudden death or disaster from the lot of His children. He stated that in Him no death can be considered pointless.

Many people misunderstand God. They expect penitence to come with a parasol to protect from storm and rain. They understand the negligent suffering, but they cannot accept it themselves or imagine why it should happen to the innocent. And they blame God and file suit against Him for it.

Would it really be good if God brought out the big cannon and bombarded evil or gave us a personal force field that bounced back every threat to our spiritual or physical security?

Think about it for a moment. Perhaps it might work for one person for a while, but let loose a million people with individualized protection, and chaos waits. The ecology of sin and salvation would mutate into aberrancy. A soldier in Vietnam accepts Christ and walks through a hail of bullets all the way to Hanoi. A criminal reads the Bible, confesses the Lord, and instantly receives a pardon.

In more than one place the Bible asserts the evenness of God. " 'What I tell you is this: Love your enemies and pray for your persecutors; only so can you be children of your heavenly Father, who makes his sun rise on good and bad alike, and sends the rain on the honest and dishonest' " (Matthew 5:44, NEB).

In the hands of an impartial God we might begin to wonder about the point of being Christian. Right now God shows partiality very seldom, and those times we call miracles. But beyond probation the Father will show us what it means to be partial. Throughout eternity He will treat us like favorite children. He will welcome us as the father welcomed the prodigal son—with the best gifts, the best of all things, deserved only because of Christ.

For the present God moves in a world beset with sin. The law of sin and death operates. Most of the time we cannot escape its consequences. Even Lazarus had to face death despite the miracle that snatched him back from it the first time. God offers no star-burst of miracle for His children, yet He constantly rebukes the accusations of Satan and keeps them Joblike as His own despite the suffering that they endure.

Think about *miracle* for a moment. It lies beyond natural law. Lazarus clambers back from the tomb —that is a miracle. A blind man sees men as if they were trees walking—that is a miracle. A lame man leaps for joy into the Temple—that is a miracle.

A world of miracles would threaten everyone's sanity. Unnatural event piled on unnatural event would make us slaves of God's whimsy rather than of His will. The laws keep on operating, and even innocence or ignorance cannot excuse the results of transgression.

It isn't much comfort to a mother of three to tell her that her husband died of cause and effect, when the accident was the fault of a drunken idiot. But physics will have its way with all of us, and the laws of motion will not be denied.

What a comfort it is to tell a person that the life that was hidden in Christ can have a new beginning. Repentance brings purpose.

It's an explanation, but no comfort, to assign the blame where it belongs in the ultimate sense, with the devil. " 'He was a murderer from the beginning, and is not rooted in the truth; there is no truth in him' " (John 8:44, NEB).

It is a comfort to know that God plans a world without Satan's evil and that God will people it with a new race free from sin. "Thus we shall always be with the Lord. Console one another, then, with these words" (1 Thessalonians 4:18, NEB).

I've heard people suggest that even if there were no life after death, Christianity would be worth it all. I don't think so. There are other systems of ethics that demand less but provide an ordered way of life. To be caught between the hither-thither waves of injustice and caprice without the promise of serene partiality at the hand of a loving Father would be an exercise in misguided morals, or at best a latter-day brand of elitist paganism.

Frankly, I'm looking forward to the time when miracles will no longer be needed and law can operate without risk to its subjects. I'm anticipating with joy the partiality of a heavenly Father freed from the restraints of a sin-cursed ecology, when He doesn't have to convince a universe of the justice of His ways, when He can do what He has always wanted to do—treat us to the storehouse of Heaven's treasure.

We catch a glimpse of what He's planning in the visions of the prophets. John spied streets of gold, bricks made of jewels, fruit that gives immortality—God isn't stingy. Who but an extravagant being could create the prolixity of nature or provide the extravaganza that is the New Jerusalem?

Perceiving the guiding hand of the Father and the ultimate kindness of Heaven, Paul informs us, "In everything, as we know, he co-operates for good with those who love God" (Romans 8:28, NEB).

Reason enough for a glad song to God.

When God
Talks Softly

In Brasilia, Oscar Niemeyer has constructed a cathedral of elegant beauty and considerable drama. Inside, its walls reach out around you in a Latin embrace. Tourists take pleasure in going to the side of the cathedral farthest from the main entrance and whispering around the curve of the wall to their friends by the door. The gentlest of sounds may be heard more than 150 feet away.

Ears tuned to quiet noises can detect them when others fail to hear. A mother hears a shuffle of the blankets and moves to her child's side in the middle of the night, while the father sleeps on.

Often a small sound or even a silence will penetrate better than a hubbub of voices. Drop some change on the floor and you have instant attention. A preacher losing attention has one sure way to revive it: simply stop preaching and remain quiet for twenty seconds.

A cacophony of communication crescendos every day around the dwellers of the modern city. It begins with commercial radio and tracks its noisy, strident way through bus, train, billboard, television, and magazine. One communication expert suggested 40,000 sense impressions in just one day for a downtowner.

How will we hear God best—in a whisper or a shout? Will we know Him best in miracle or meditation, parade or prayer?

Ancient Israel thought they understood and heard God best in the shout. Their knowledge of Him began with the plagues of Egypt. It moved with swiftness from the death of the firstborn to the hissing walls of water that hemmed their walk through the Red Sea. When drinking water turned sour or failed completely, a miracle put the matter straight. And every day fresh food appeared from nowhere. They moved constantly in the milieu of miracles.

But they had even more to see of all that God was capable of when they came to Sinai. Here God forever grooved the racial memory of the Jewish race. They never could forget and never have forgotten the moment of splendor when God spoke to them in person.

"On the third day, when morning came, there were peals of thunder and flashes of lightning, dense cloud on the mountain and a loud trumpet blast; the people in the camp were all terrified. Moses brought the people out of the camp to meet God, and they took their stand at the foot of the mountain. Mount Sinai was all smoking because the Lord had come down upon it in fire; the smoke went up like the smoke of a kiln; all the people were terrified, and the sound of the trumpet grew ever louder. Whenever Moses spoke, God answered him in a peal of thunder" (Exodus 19:16-19, NEB).

To those who have watched the sound and light presentation at the pyramids of Egypt, the Red Fort in Delhi, or some other historical site, a tiny fragment of that day at Sinai has entered the awareness. Yet this was a sound and light demonstration, an audiovisual multimedia presentation that defies all the technology of this communication era.

Three million people surged against the base of the mountain. The pageant began with lightning and thunder and a smoking mountain. Then God turned up the volume and a trumpet blast reverberated from unseen instruments. An earthquake shook the earth and brought terror to the people. Every crag and crevice poured out smoke. Over it all the trumpet announced the event in louder and louder tones. Then the thunder took on new significance. No longer was it answering the lightning. Now it replied to the voice of Moses. Suddenly the people knew whom they were hearing. God, the I AM, the One who had brought them out of Egypt, was speaking to them in their language, and they could understand Him.

"I am the Lord your God who brought you out of Egypt, out of the land of slavery" (Exodus 20:2, NEB). On and on the voice went, defining principles of relationship between God and man and man and man that have defied emulation from that day to this.

The race of Israel never forgot. "Did any people ever hear the voice of God speaking out of the fire, as you heard it, and remain alive?" (Deuteronomy 4:33, NEB). Twenty-eight times Moses calls the people to "hear the voice" in his farewell sermon in the Book of Deuteronomy. And his plea echoes again and again in the prophets' writings and even in the New Testament. A God who speaks to His people, not by the ones or twos, but by the millions, can never be forgotten or ignored.

At first thought this seems the natural, normal way for God to operate. Omniscience, omnipotence, and omnipresence provide a logical background for miracle and might. Without this, Israel could never have distinguished between the true God and the tribal deities of the surrounding tribes. Without it even sophisticated moderns might find it hard to know who God is.

Now take a step further. Picture a world moving toward a destined end. Not just millions, but billions wait to be warned. How to do it? Re-create Sinai? Come down to Sinai and Fuji and Matterhorn and Pike's Peak and show Hollywood how it's really done? Not in the last-day context, for that's the way the devil will work. "These spirits were devils, with power to work miracles" (Revelation 16:14, NEB). Only when Christ returns to earth the second time will He replay Sinai, and then He will do it on a worldwide scale. "Then God's temple in heaven was laid open, and within the temple was seen the ark of his covenant. There came flashes of lightning and peals of thunder, an earthquake, and a storm of hail" (Revelation 11:19, NEB).

Though Israel never forgot the experience of Sinai, and it ultimately led them toward a true understanding of the nature of God and laid the basis for the coming of Christ and the Christian gospel, the immediate effect shows one of the dangers of miracles. Unless the heart prepares itself with a faith that will survive the return to humdrum living after the hour of majesty, belief in God may actually suffer.

We might best describe what happened to Israel as a "wonderholic" effect. They looked around for the next wonder. The human heart longs for the shout of God—a trumpet blast, a voice that speaks of transcending power, an act so unquestionably His that it can have no other explanation, a public presentation defying the explanations of science or the musings of philosophy.

Days passed. Moses had gone into the smoke which still hung over the mountain. Would he ever return, or had he died there from the glory of the Lord? When nothing happened, they wondered about Moses' God—He was still only that; they had not accepted Him as their personal Saviour yet—they considered the alternate deities that might now lead them to new wonders. Did Aaron also have a god? What if they tried the gods the Egyptians worshiped? Hence the golden calf: " 'These . . . are your gods, O Israel, that brought you up from Egypt' " (Exodus 32:4, NEB).

Once caught by the wonderholic effect, it becomes hard to shake. It may even become a weapon to attack divinity. Fourteen hundred years after Sinai the Pharisees saw Christ raise the dead, heal the sick, feed the five thousand, and ascribed it all to the devil. Taking another tack, they pestered Him for further miracles to substantiate the ones already performed.

Trying to make God perform on cue goes along with other ways men try to manipulate God. But He would not let Himself be carved in an image because He knew mankind would use that object to manipulate Him to their advantage. He would not let Himself be put in a box from which He could break out only by another miracle. Not far from this lies the presumption on God's goodness which places itself in a position from which it challenges God to break it free.

Like the Phoenician priests on Carmel, this places God afar off, asleep, or busy if He isn't performing on cue. A modern who waves a flag at God by triple tithing, strict conformity, or bouts of fanaticism isn't all that far from the slashing knives of Mt. Carmel.

We need the miracle worker of Sinai. We need the consciousness of Omnipotence working wonders in the world. What we must guard against is the conclusion that God is working only when He shouts. We also need to understand that *miracle* is something that operates outside of law and over law. Once Christ established salvation on the cross, the spiritual laws that govern eternal life took over. Premised on the sacrifice of Calvary, forgiveness, justification, cleansing, sanctification, are laws and not miracles. Putting them in any other perspective places the sinner in danger of relying on feeling rather than fact, sight rather than surety.

And will we hear when God speaks softly?

God talks quietly most of the time. We hear Him through the Word, through prayer, through the Spirit. It takes much faith to accept a miracle and then go back to the whispering voice of Love.

Carmel's miracle united Israel in a chant of triumph: "The Lord, he is God!" Elijah capitalized on the victory by slaying the priests of Jezebel, but hours later he fled from her like a whipped cur.

Directions

God led him to Sinai, back to Moses' mountain. Back to the summit that once smoked to hide the brightness of the Almighty. And God played back Moses' experience for Elijah.

"He rose and ate and drank and, sustained by this food, he went on for forty days and forty nights to Horeb, the mount of God. . . .

"Suddenly the word of the Lord came to him: 'Why are you here, Elijah?' 'Because of my great zeal for the Lord the God of Hosts,' he said. . . . 'I alone am left, and they seek to take my life.' The answer came: 'Go and stand on the mount before the Lord.' For the Lord was passing by: a great and strong wind came rending mountains and shattering rocks before him, but the Lord was not in the wind; and after the wind there was an earthquake, but the Lord was not in the earthquake; and after the earthquake fire, but the Lord was not in the fire; and after the fire a low murmuring sound" (1 Kings 19:8-13, NEB).

Comes the real question of Elijah's life: Could he believe the whisper as much as the shout? Must it always be Carmel and Sinai? or could it be the susurrus of the Spirit? Elijah heard, believed, and acted on faith, and he joined Moses with Christ on another mountain—the Mount of Transfiguration.

Must we live on wonders? or can we hear the whispering of God? Learning to be satisfied with the assurance of a written promise leads us closer to God's way of working than does expecting a wonder. Begging a miracle may make mockery of the assurances the Spirit gives through His Word. Accepting a miracle as a strength to faith takes us nearer to our Redeemer.

Something marvelous is happening to Christians in the Philippines. A devil departs from a headhunter in New Guinea. A thousand youth accept baptism in Rwanda. A friend rises from a terminal illness, restored. And I? I am left with a pain that never ceases, a child who scorns the Lord, a victory that mirages away from me. Then I must listen for the still, small voice of pen and Presence.

How much the Christian needs the Bible! From its pages we know that real people knew miracles. The Bible tells that miracles happen and that they don't happen; and we need to learn both truths.

How easy to be an Elijah arguing with the Lord, "Because of my great zeal . . ." Or an Aaron justifying false concepts of God, "These be your gods. . . ." How hard to learn that God yields neither to bullying nor competition.

Yet faith fits easily to the quiet moments of Nicodemus' talking with the Master. *That* we can all do. Come in lowliness, seeking only what God is ready to give, and then say to the Giver, "It is enough, Lord."

"God himself has said, 'I will never leave you or desert you'; and so we can take courage and say, 'The Lord is my helper, I will not fear; what can man do to me?' " (Hebrews 13:5, 6, NEB).

King Waves
Kill

"Police have issued a warning to all anglers to exercise the greatest of care when fishing from the rocks around the south coast. Visiting sightseers are urged to be very careful when climbing or standing on some of the rocky outcrops along the coast. Previous experience has shown that the risk of being swept off the rocks by a huge wave—a king wave—is ever present."

Despite warnings these king waves still claim lives as tourists and fishermen venture onto the cliffs and rugged rocks of the south coast of Western Australia. The swells of the Indian Ocean crash against this coast during storms. Waves up to one hundred feet high sweep over the precipices in cascades of foam. No one would venture near the power of the sea on those days. Even on a fine day the water sends plumes of spray and cones of water up over the rocky outcrops.

Most local inhabitants enjoy the beauty from a distance and with a sober respect. Not only when storms are rolling in from the South Pole does caution impose itself. In the leading daily newspaper of the state these words appeared: "It is important to remember that no matter what the weather conditions are or how safe a fishing spot may seem, the sea can become a relentless foe, defying everything devised or attempted by man to effect a rescue."

On a bright, sunny afternoon, with no hint of storm, Albert Harrison, a professional fisherman, picked up his brother, Leslie, for a fishing trip to the Skippy Rocks, fifteen miles from Albany. They chose a familiar and perfectly safe spot. High and dry, it offered an easy escape route. As professionals they knew the danger and had no intention of being caught by a king wave.

With their backs to a small rock, they enjoyed the warm sun while their lines dangled into the water sixty feet below. The muted thunder of the waves below lulled any thoughts of danger.

But out of the depths of the ocean an incredibly huge wave was rearing itself. For a moment it held them hypnotized by the crest that loomed level with their rock, then roared in on them with the thunder of a rocket blast. Tons of water swirled around them, burying and driving them. Then the drag of those tons of water pulled them relentlessly toward the cliff's edge.

The tumbling torrent prohibited walking or running and made standing hopeless. They clung to outcrops, gashed their fingers and hands as the water tore them loose, and lost the battle in a final choking plunge to the ocean below.

We know the story because, through some freak of wave and water, Leslie escaped—one of very few to survive a king wave.

Lungs bursting, he struggled against the forces that sought to tie him to the ocean floor. Then the next wave reversed the thrust and popped him through the surface, only to drive him shoreward and under again. Wave after wave fought for his life, either sucking him under or hurling him toward the rocks. In a moment of clarity he decided to head for the open sea, using the backward drag of the water to help him, and that saved his life.

Aided by a current paralleling the coast, he struggled beyond the wavebreak and along the shore where the waves rolled him to a sandy cove.

Albert was never seen again.

Just a year before the Harrison tragedy two young schoolteachers, Janice Bye and Wendy Lefroy, twenty and nineteen respectively, lost their lives near a local tourist attraction called the Natural Bridge. Apparently the ocean claimed them when they clambered down under the bridge, still a good forty feet above the sea's surface, to photograph the sea through the arch of the bridge. Only their car nearby offered an answer to this mystery of the sea.

Signs near this spot spell the warning: "Dangerous Coast—King Waves Kill." That very morning fellow campers had joked with the girls as they left for a day of sightseeing, "Don't get washed off the rocks."

Similar hazards threaten life on many coasts. Recently a young Seventh-day Adventist preacher took a group of children to look at the scenery around Signal Hill near St. John's, Newfoundland. They climbed down toward the ocean and watched at a respectable distance as it pummeled the coast.

Like the Harrisons, they had no chance to run when a wave swept in on them. The minister grabbed two of the children. A third was almost lost, but his fingers jammed in a crevice and saved him.

Off the Cape of Good Hope huge waves menace shipping. Charts warn of these swells of sudden and unexpected proportions. One huge tanker got its back broken when a wave crested and left the ship balancing on its ridge.

What creates these huge waves? Oceanographers record their existence and theorize. They know that at unspecified times a seemingly regular pattern will be interrupted by one giant wave. This is not to be confused with the usual big wave in a series of swells. King waves defy any prediction. Some think Western Australia's waves may form when huge chunks of ice break off from the glaciers of Antarctica. Others point to the deep trough off the coast and think that a freak coincidence of wave and current, funneled and boosted by this gash in the ocean floor, forces the waves shoreward.

Looking at the spiritual world, Paul had a parallel in mind when he said, "If you feel sure that you are standing firm, beware! You may fall" (1 Corinthians 10:12, NEB). Consider Samson, swept off the rock of his Nazarite vow by the wiles of a temptress. David felt secure in the newfound safety of his kingdom but fell an easy prey to Bathsheba's charms. Hezekiah thought it no harm to show the Babylonians the wonders of his achievements as king. Ananias and Sapphira did not even feel the wave of greed that rose within them as they deceived Peter.

One of the tragedies of alcohol lies in the uncertainty of its victims. Even more tragic than its effect on health or its leeching of the pocketbook is alcoholism, the self-inflicted disease that gives no clues to its next addict.

Little Ralph de Jesus, the twelve-year-old witness to a drug commission, told of his experience, "Everyone I knew was taking dope. I had to find a way I could get it, too, so that I could be part of the local scene. Actually, it wasn't even hard to get drugs. You have to fight off those who are pushing them. Soon I was robbing to get money for a fix."

Anyone resisting the social pressures of his peers knows how the king waves rise around those who demur. Often the victim has no intention of being hooked—once will be enough to know what it's like.

Diane Linkletter fell to a simple enough reaction. Confused by minor psychological problems, she decided to trip out on LSD, thinking it might help her. Long after the physical residues of the drug had left her system, she was wrestling with the overwhelming psychological nightmares the psychedelic induced.

She tried the drug once more. Fighting unimaginable foes, she walked through the open window of a sixth-floor apartment.

"It wasn't suicide," announced her television-personality father, Art Linkletter, "because she wasn't herself. It was murder. She was murdered by the people who manufacture and sell LSD."

One wonders how much richer and better society would be if all addictive products could be kept from their potential victims. The cost to society of tobacco-, alcohol-, and drug-related crimes and illnesses far exceeds their tax or employment values.

Vernon Slider, a television executive in Philadelphia, told of his life in an ad paid for by his company. "I think I had rather a novel childhood for the west side of Fresno. I got drunk when I was nine, and by the time I was fourteen I was smoking pot, and by the time I was sixteen I was a full-fledged member of the drug-addicted world. . . . When I got to San Quentin at the age of 21, and I saw some changes, and I saw some people, and I saw things that went on down there that was unbelievable.

"About fourteen hours in that jailhouse being locked up, I think the full realization came to me. Hey, you're not going to get any more heroin today. And let me tell you my body went through some changes that in order for you to fully appreciate it, you would have had to have been there. . . . So I laid in the middle of a cell in a stinking county jail and literally died, . . . and I laid on the cell floor for fourteen days in that position with people walking around me, and they felt about as much compassion for me as you do for your worst enemy."

Here's a struggle more violent than escape from a king wave.

Slider tells this about his childhood: "I didn't have heroes like young people have. I think this is one of the things that led to my addiction to heroin —the lack of identity. I didn't have an identity" (*Broadcasting*, March 9, 1970, p. 18).

I still continue to marvel that people like Ralph de Jesus and Vernon Slider can fight free of addiction. Yet this promise surfaces more than once in the Bible: "So far you have faced no trial beyond what man can bear. God keeps faith, and he will not allow you to be tested above your powers, but when the test comes he will at the same time provide a way out, by enabling you to sustain it" (1 Corinthians 10:13, NEB).

So many people are innocently caught up with physical-addiction problems. Social pressure creates addicts. Joel Fort surveyed twenty school districts around Berkeley, California, and reported that 75 percent of the children had tried alcohol, 20 percent habitually. Forty percent used marijuana and considerable numbers, the so-called hard drugs.

At a less-dramatic level countless millions fight battles with tobacco, coffee, and other drugs against which society levels no strictures. On the spiritual level a bad temper, a stubborn will, an uncontrollable libido, destroy Christian faith in many lives.

A look at the processes of temptation helps us understand what we face and shows us ways of escape. "Temptation arises when a man is enticed and lured away by his own lust; then lust conceives, and gives birth to sin; and sin full-grown breeds death" (James 1:14, 15, NEB). God does not tempt nor permit temptation. Temptation begins either with habit, proximity, or availability. The mind creates a picture of a different state induced by yielding to the temptation. Lucifer, the angel who became Satan, went through this process: "For thou hast said in thine heart, I will ascend into heaven, I will exalt my throne above the stars of God: . . . I will ascend above the heights of the clouds; I will be like the most High" (Isaiah 14:13, 14, KJV).

All temptations since then have followed the same route. Even the sudden, overwhelming impulse has this route.

Only as we loathe the condition temptation produces, yearn for escape from its bonds, and recognize our powerlessness to break free can God begin to help. It's no use saying, "The devil made me do it," even though we know he is the root of all temptation. Excuses gloss, rather than reveal, our true condition.

Through Christ help comes. "Every temptation that has come your way is the kind that normally comes to people. But God keeps his promise, and he will not allow you to be tempted beyond your power to resist; at the time you are tempted he will give you the strength to endure it, and so provide you with a way out" (1 Corinthians 10:13, TEV).

Habit plays a large part in temptation. Once the mind or body has grown used to the transition from one state to another and has walked over the barriers and through the warning signals time and again, it may find that route far easier to follow than resistance. Proximity to the temptation stimulus, especially one that has been used over and over again, is an almost certain prelude to a fall. There's nothing smart or brave about putting oneself near the stimulus that has prompted temptation. "Awake! be on the alert! Your enemy the devil, like a roaring lion, prowls round looking for someone to devour" (1 Peter 5:8, NEB).

Christ offers help to those who know their need. Peter's cry, "Lord, save me," has its answer. "And so he is able, now and always, to save those who come to God through him, because he lives forever to plead with God for them" (Hebrews 7:25, TEV).

Satan does more than tempt us. He utilizes the act of sin or the yielding to a habit as a way to make us more susceptible in the future. He accuses us of weakness, of unworthiness, of worthlessness. Satan is also the accuser of the brethren. To know he has been vanquished through Calvary is a vast advantage Christians possess as they struggle with temptation and sin. "Then I heard a voice in heaven proclaiming aloud: 'This is the hour of victory for our God, the hour of his sovereignty and power, when his Christ comes to his rightful rule! For the accuser of our brothers is overthrown, who day and night accused them before our God' " (Revelation 12:10, NEB).

Temptation need not be a king wave to sweep us off the rock of our salvation. The promises of God hold out assurance of safety to those who trust.

Perhaps the most important lesson to learn is that where we take our stand determines our fate.

"Stand firm, I say. Fasten on the belt of truth; for coat of mail put on integrity; let the shoes on your feet be the gospel of peace, to give you firm footing; and, with all these, take up the great shield of faith, with which you will be able to quench all the flaming arrows of the evil one. Take salvation for helmet; for sword, take that which the Spirit gives you—the words that come from God" (Ephesians 6:14-17, NEB).

The Best Time of All

Celebration!—"Open to me the gates of victory; I will enter by them and praise the Lord."

Procession!—"This is the gate of the Lord; the victors shall make their entry through it."

Praise!—"I will praise thee, for thou hast answered me and hast become my deliverer."

Exultation!—"This is the day on which the Lord has acted: let us exult and rejoice in it" (Psalm 118:19, 20, 21, 24, NEB).

We waited by the procession route to watch Queen Elizabeth go by. All the city joined us in celebration. We caught one glimpse of a smiling, gracious face, then raced across the city by back streets for another, and then another. Our monarch was with us, and this was reason to rejoice.

Celebration shines brightness into dull lives. Birthdays, anniversaries, graduations, give us cause to be glad. Celebration remembers time and event. Something good happened; we recall it, and we celebrate.

Celebration marks the end of wars. Even the vanquished find a gladness at the end of a struggle. A great man's passing is marked through the years, and we honor him in celebration.

Though we may probe theology, ponder prophecy, or analyze doctrine, if we overlook celebration we have missed an important facet of the Bible's message.

One may hear it in Paul's words: "Rejoice evermore"; or in John's paean: " 'Great and marvellous are thy deeds, O Lord God, sovereign over all' "; or in the blind man's glow: " 'All I know is this: once I was blind, now I can see.' " Christ banished mourning, lamentation, depression, from the future of mankind. For those who look upward in faith much of the joy of the future can arrive in this life. On the cross and through the empty tomb Jesus created new life, new hope, new creatures. "Who is there to rescue me out of this body doomed to death? God alone, through Jesus Christ our Lord! Thanks be to God!" (Romans 7:25, NEB).

Earth began with shouting and singing "when the morning stars sang together and all the sons of God shouted aloud" (Job 38:7, NEB). It will end in praise: " 'Amen! Praise and glory and wisdom, thanksgiving and honour, power and might, be to our God for ever and ever! Amen' " (Revelation 7:12, NEB).

The saved life does many things to show its condition. It acknowledges forgiveness, it knows redemption, it senses victory; but it also celebrates God and His goodness in Christ.

Consider the days of Creation. Angels watch spellbound as the Creator unveils His new masterpiece. Worlds afar wonder at the immense variety of plant and animal life. Created lords of distant realms delight in the ecology of Eden. All anticipate the next step. For them it is a reliving of the birth of their own planets, the creation of their own environments. Now comes the supreme moment, Whom would God make to rule the new world? What would he be like?

Memories of other creations, of the added wealth God gave in past acts, turn toward the Maker as He shapes man and then stoops down to breathe life into the still form. Intellects reach out with God for the new intelligence, and there is instant rapport. God has done it again; this new being is just right, his place in the divine scheme needed and known. There had been no lack before, but now there is need for man, and God has given him to the universe. Then, "Alleluia! Alleluia!" Angels and all created beings join shouts of praise and songs of gladness. An earth is born in celebration.

"So it was; and God saw all that he had made, and it was very good. . . . On the sixth day God completed all the work he had been doing, and on the seventh day he ceased from all his work. God blessed the seventh day and made it holy, because on that day he ceased from all the work he had set himself to do" (Genesis 1:31–2:3, NEB).

Hear the new voice joining the symphony of the stars, the voice of a new creation, Adam, adding a new tone to the universal choir—the song had never been so sweet, the harmony so complete.

This was the song of the first Sabbath, and the benevolent Father joined with His creation and marveled at the goodness of the unity it brought. How could anyone forget that moment? From that time on it was to carry with it, in the day God gave, the remembrance of the rejoicing of the universe at the creation of a world and its ruler.

Even sin was not to wipe away the memory of that glad day. God set the sequence of days indelibly in the customs and history of humanity so that the Sabbath would not be forgotten.

Yet men did forget, not the weekly cycle but the significance of the seventh day. Not all of them forgot. Adam lived through generations of antediluvians and testified to Creation and its weekly memorial. Could he ever forget awakening to the music of Creation? Could he expunge the memories of evening strolls with God? Who could distort his memories or argue his experience? And always, week by week, the Sabbath came to remind him of his first moments, the sudden vision of God bending over him in love, watching his waking, touching his mind with reassurance.

Whatever man might think or do, there never has been any way God could change the celebration of Creation. He fixed it as a farmer fixes a post against which a whole fence might strain. The Sabbath stands as the cornerpost of faith, the fixed point in man's experience from which all subsequent events, doctrines, and teachings take their direction and strength.

This then is God's command to celebrate: "Remember to keep the sabbath day holy. You have six days to labour and do all your work. But the seventh day is a sabbath of the Lord your God; that day you shall not do any work, you, your son or your daughter, your slave or your slave-girl, your cattle or the alien within your gates; for in six days the Lord made heaven and earth, the sea, and all that is in them, and on the seventh day he rested. Therefore the Lord blessed the sabbath day and declared it holy" (Exodus 20:8-11, NEB).

Note the parameters of celebration God decrees. The operative word is *rest*. Yet this is not the equivalent of doing nothing. Rest means the human equal of what God did, blessing and sanctifying the Sabbath. The Sabbath gives time for praising and blessing the name of God. Here is a day to change activities, a day of forgetfulness of the routine and tension of living, a day to accept the fellowship and communion of God and His people. It is a day for sanctified or holy activities, for stopping secular acts and beginning sacred ones. A day to go to church, to meet in worship, to join in hymns.

Nothing should blight the gladness of God's day of rest. From the moment we match our sequence with the divine and begin our rest when the sun sets on Friday, as He did at Creation, we enter special time in which He has placed special blessing. Thus we share the divine intention that this should be a day to be glad in.

"If you cease to tread the sabbath underfoot, and keep my holy day free from your own affairs, if you call the sabbath a day of joy and the Lord's holy day a day to be honoured, if you honour it by not plying your trade, not seeking your own interest or attending to your own affairs, then you shall find your joy in the Lord, and I will set you riding on the heights of the earth" (Isaiah 58:13, 14, NEB).

Yet this is only half the picture.

"All that came to be was alive with his life, and that life was the light of men" (John 1:3, 4, NEB). "The life I now live is not my life, but the life which Christ lives in me" (Galatians 2:20, NEB).

If celebration is right for the birth of a world, it is right for the re-creation of spiritual life. " 'I tell you, there is joy among the angels of God over one sinner who repents' " (Luke 15:10, NEB). Heaven attaches great import to the rebirth of a life. At the moment that life reaches toward God and accepts Him as Lord and Saviour, then joy breaks out in heaven just as it did at the making of a world. At that moment the sinner finds rest from his labors and God takes over. God rejoices; the sinner rejoices—a celebration!

Ezekiel saw the clear connection between creation and re-creation: "Further, I gave them my sabbaths as a sign between us, so that they should know that I, the Lord, was hallowing them for myself" (Ezekiel 20:12, NEB). Just as God used a day to hallow a creation to Himself, so He uses the same day to hallow lives to Himself. Jesus rested in the grave on the Sabbath as God had rested in Creation, thereby reminding us that in Him all mankind may have spiritual rest.

A restless age seeks for peace of mind. We need rest from sins, rest from labor, rest from a disordered world. God has promised all three for the life that yields to His creative power. These three goals have always been God's intention. God promised Israel rest in Canaan. Joshua failed to give them that rest (Hebrews 4). But God has not forgotten that promise of rest. It awaits His people in the new earth. God promised rest from labor, and we can choose that today as the faithful did in the past, by resting on the Sabbath. And most important of all He assures us of spiritual rest.

For all three rests the Sabbath is a token, a sign, a symbol. "Therefore, a Sabbath rest still awaits the people of God; for anyone who enters God's rest, rests from his own work as God did from his. Let us then make every effort to enter that rest, so that no one may fall by following this evil example of unbelief'' (Hebrews 4:9-11, NEB).

The Sabbath is both the Lord's day and man's day. "The Sabbath was made for the sake of man and not man for the Sabbath: therefore the Son of Man is sovereign even over the Sabbath" (Mark 2:27, 28, NEB). As its sovereign, Jesus kept it holy (Luke 4:16). As its Lord, He used it to create happiness and renewal (John 9:15; Luke 4:31-37).

Whoever comes to the new earth of God's elect will celebrate the Sabbath. "For, as the new heavens and the new earth which I am making shall endure in my sight, says the Lord, so shall your race and your name endure; and month by month at the new moon, and week by week on the sabbath, all mankind shall come to bow down before me, says the Lord" (Isaiah 66:22, 23, NEB).

Thus God sets our faith in the future as He has done in the past. If He could come to the end of the work of Creation, proclaim it good, and celebrate with the Sabbath, then He will also come to the end of the work of remaking, proclaim it good, and celebrate with the Sabbath. And as the Sabbath on this world shows the power of God to create and redeem, so in the new earth it will draw all His children to an act of celebration for the re-creating, redeeming love of Christ.

Like the farmer with his cornerposts, God sets a second one in the new earth. He strains the fence of truth against the Sabbath in Eden and the Sabbath in the new earth. And the line runs straight between. All spiritual truth, all doctrine, measures against the truth of the Sabbath. Without a creating, redeeming God no doctrine would be true or any truth a doctrine. The Sabbath says to man all he needs to know about God. It speaks of Him as creating, personal, loving, sharing. And when you have said that about God, you have also said Calvary, the Holy Spirit, eternal life, forgiveness, and sanctification.

"Skin Seven-day"

Luke, a black-skinned Solomon Islander, was talking with his Papuan friend. They spoke in the lingua franca of the Melanesian Islands—pidgin English. With a little help in spelling and anglicizing, it went like this:

"Him he good feller?" Luke asked. "Him he seven-day?"

"Him he seven-day all right. Him he baptize finish long three feller Christmas."

But Luke wasn't satisfied with that answer. He wanted to know the real condition of the third party. He persisted, "Him he good feller?"

The other dark head shook slowly, "No, no, him skin seven-day, that's all."

Skin seven-day? What kind of a Seventh-day Adventist could that be?

"House belong him he got bad feller picture, plenty tobacco he stop along house belong him; he fight im mary belong him; he no go along house belong God."

In other words this nameless friend was a fake. A skin seven-day with a veneer of religion but no real practice of it. Seventh-day Adventist Christians are known the world over for their high standards. One who claims the name but not the way of life is as much out of place in New Guinea as in New York.

"Consistency thou art a jewel." How often we fail to present in private what we profess in public.

Jesus Christ had words to describe it: " 'Hypocrites! You are like whitewashed tombs, which look fine on the outside, but are full of dead men's bones and rotten stuff on the inside. In the same way, on the outside you appear to everybody as good, but inside you are full of hypocrisy and sins' " (Matthew 23:27, 28, TEV).

One of the specific signs of the time of the end will be religious put-ons. They will fool those seeking direction in life and offer false impressions and false teachings.

Among the Jews of Christ's day many claimed special messages from God. Some even believed or taught that they were the Messiah. A nation that received many direct messages from God through the prophets stood open to deception.

Jesus warned, " 'Then, if anyone says to you, "Look, here is the Messiah", or, "There he is", do not believe it. Imposters will come claiming to be messiahs or prophets, and they will produce great signs and wonders to mislead God's chosen, if such a thing were possible. See, I have forewarned you. If they tell you, "He is there in the wilderness", do not go out; or if they say, "He is there in the inner room", do not believe it' " (Matthew 24:23-26, NEB).

How can one tell the real from the fake? We live in the times Jesus spoke of and we must expect that more attempts to deceive and delude will occur. The

Bible gives certain general definitions.

"Who is the liar? Who but he that denies that Jesus is the Christ? He is Antichrist, for he denies both the Father and the Son: to deny the Son is to be without the Father; to acknowledge the Son is to have the Father too" (1 John 2:22, 23, NEB).

Despite the appeal of the Hare Krishna movement with its jingling bells, saffron robes, and authoritarian creed, not too many people are going to join the jiving youngsters parading city streets and chanting their way to fulfillment. Nor are swamis and gurus going to deceive large numbers with mystic sayings and meditative rituals.

The greatest danger comes from our own attitudes. Satan will make himself appear like an angel of light. He will have the world wondering after him. His best deceptions will be those that march near the banner of truth.

The peaches gradually developed toward perfection. Already we could taste the fulfillment of our months of faithfulness in spraying and pruning. A soft blush was spreading across the fruit on the sunward bough.

With eager hands we reached for the tender fruit. A quick bite. A look of disbelief. A great deal of spitting. What had gone wrong? Our preparations took no account of the ubiquitous fruit fly that makes a slimy, maggotty mess of the most succulent-looking fruit. Before taking a bite, only the practiced eye could detect where maggot began and good fruit ended.

It doesn't take too long for the innocence of childhood to find masks to hide its real feelings. As one grows older, masks seem essential for mental survival. Society imposes—even demands—inhibitions on our actions. We end up seething inside but conforming outside.

Society requires a mask; Christianity suggests a robe. The patina of propriety that many achieve is a long way from the presence of Christ in the life. Yet the discerning eye of divinity sees through.

"At that moment the disciples came to Jesus, asking, 'Who is the greatest in the Kingdom of heaven?' Jesus called a child, had him stand in front of them, and said, 'Remember this! Unless you change and become like children, you will never enter the Kingdom of heaven. The greatest in the Kingdom of heaven is the one who humbles himself and becomes like this child' " (Matthew 18:1-4, TEV).

To close the credibility gap the Christian must put off self and put on Christ. Conversion peels off the crust of sin and reveals the soft whiteness of forgiveness and surrender.

Then and then only does the outside agree with the inside. "There is no condemnation now for those who live in union with Christ Jesus. . . . God did this so that the righteous demands of the law might be fully satisfied in us who live according to the Spirit, not according to human nature" (Romans 8:1-4, TEV).

The reservoir of Christian ethics and moral uprightness is fast running out. We deplore its passing, but in a way the world is better without it. Many people are fooled by comparing themselves with the neighborhood moralist and deciding that they are as good as he. Comparison is no substitute for conversion. It threatens individual salvation far more than all the gurus the East can muster. A moralistic society devoid of Christian belief makes people satisfied with morals. That's why Paul reiterates his conclusion that "there is none righteous, no, not one."

Hyprocrisy usually points the finger at someone else. It compares practice with profession. When the two do not coincide, hypocrisy is defined. Yet hypocrisy recognizes the fact that there is a standard. To be without hypocrites in a sinful world would be a dangerous plight. The aware hypocrite at least knows where he should be. Those who point out hypocrisy discern the difference between the real and phony. As long as the real is recognized for what it is there is hope for change.

Hypocrisy is more than the inability of a person to match acts to aspirations. Satisfaction with the double standard marks the hypocrite. Paul was no hypocrite when he said, "I do not understand what I do; for I don't do what I would like to do, but instead I do what I hate" (Romans 7:15, TEV). Paul was expressing human weakness. His life trend was toward God. "My inner being delights in the law of God. But I see a different law at work in my body —a law that fights against the law that my mind approves of" (verses 22, 23, TEV).

A trader in Sri Lanka sold me two brown ebony elephants a few years ago. The deep black and brown grain of the wood, made lustrous with much rubbing, delighted both touch and eye. It took several seasons to reveal the deception in the carvings. On the underside of one of the elephants a deep scar formed. Looking closer I saw that wax had been pushed into the scar, colored, and then polished along with the timber.

What then is the spiritual solution?

The Christian need have no doubt as to his condition.

"So sin must no longer reign in your mortal body, exacting obedience to the body's desires. You must no longer put its several parts at sin's disposal, as implements for doing wrong. No: put yourselves at the disposal of God, as dead men raised to life; yield your bodies to him as implements for doing right; for sin shall no longer be your master, because you are no longer under law, but under the grace of God" (Romans 6:12-14, NEB).

Sincerity does not need the wax of legalism to gloss discrepancies. Only the surrendered, yielded Christian lives the life of sincerity. The solution lies in surrender.

Yet nothing is more devastating to faith than assuming that *all* externals are a put-on. Many people stay away from Christ because they confuse the ideal with the real and therefore expect Christians to arrive readyborn perfect. If someone doesn't live up to their expectations of what a Christian is, they get disgusted and scorn Christianity.

Many go to visit the mission outreaches of Christianity with thoughts of rice Christians in their minds. A few years ago my own visit to India raised this suspicion. Could it be that the work of the church had, in fact, been built around the purchase of belief by offers of work, food, or money?

Some of this went on—at least in the thinking of the benefited. However, I was answered differently in one experience.

The small village of Avrampatty lies near Dindigul in south India. Many years ago the British faced a severe test of their administration of the Indian colony. One tribe had a reputation of being robbers. Wandering like gypsies, they battened on the troubles of others, robbing the helpless, murdering where the price was right. They were opportunists of the worst kind. To keep track of the tribe the British declared it criminal. From that time on every member of that tribe was a criminal, no matter what the record might say otherwise.

With the coming of independence the Indian government gave members of the tribe a piece of land, removed the stigma, and ordered them to build a village and settle down.

They couldn't doff their reputation overnight. But they had help. A pair of Christian layworkers visited the village. They brought nothing but their faith in Jesus Christ, and that was enough. Today many people of this village worship in the little Adventist church I visited.

Here are some ways to check off relationships with Christ. Paul said, "Put yourselves to the test and judge yourselves, to find out whether you are living in the faith. Surely you know that Christ Jesus is in you?—unless you have completely failed" (2 Corinthians 13:5, TEV). How close do we come to these concepts?

1. "The life I now live is not my life, but the life which Christ lives in me" (Galatians 2:20, NEB).

2. "Pray without ceasing" (1 Thessalonians 5:17, KJV).

3. "Adapt yourselves no longer to the pattern of this present world, but let your minds be remade and your whole nature thus transformed" (Romans 12:2, NEB).

4. "And now, my friends, all that is true, all that is noble, all that is just and pure, all that is lovable and gracious, whatever is excellent and admirable

—fill your thoughts with these things" (Philippians 4:8, NEB).

Being human is making mistakes; being Christian is having help to overcome them. The biggest mistake is donning the cloak of Christianity before the robe of Christ's righteousness.

God has never asked for goodness first. He has just one request—"My son, give me thine heart."

So Many Ways
to End
the World

News from the world's scientists offers yet another nightmare ending for life on planet Earth. We've been told over and over that a nuclear war might snuff out millions of lives through radiation. Now a new look at the fragile ecology of spaceship Earth discombobulates us with a threat that would eliminate all life with much less than full-scale war; in fact, it might not even need war at all.

Ozone, a form of oxygen, hangs above us in a protective layer some ten to thirty miles up. It shields the planet from ultraviolet rays, which are great for a summer tan in the small quantities that penetrate the ozone shield but deadly in their unmitigated form.

Supersonic jets may break up the ozone, according to a chemist at the University of California at Berkeley. As these jets traverse high altitudes they emit large quantities of oxides of nitrogen. Oxides of nitrogen react with ozone in producing ordinary oxygen, thus destroying ozone. If enough of these oxides spread through the ozone layer, it might disintegrate completely. Some scientists suggest that as few as 500 supersonics flying regular routes would devastate the protective layer.

A limited nuclear war would compound the problem. The mushroom clouds of atomic explosions carry with them huge quantities of oxides of nitrogen, which spread through the stratosphere. A sudden rash of such explosions in a nuclear war might nibble away the stability of the ozone layer (*Newsweek*, September 16, 1974, p. 57).

Thus humanity demonstrates its instinct for cutting its own jugular.

On the same page of *Newsweek* is another article predicting doom. While it may be a "heyyear" for astrologers, 1982 looms as a harbinger of disaster in the minds of many astronomers. Following a 179-year cycle, 1982 puts all the planets in line with the sun, thus exerting exceptional gravitational pulls which will affect both the sun and its satellites.

Huge solar flares, drawn upward by extra gravitation, will disrupt the upper atmosphere of the earth, creating freak weather patterns. These changes will whip up winds of abnormal velocity as well as rainfall and temperature changes. The whole effect may be to vary the frictional effect of the atmosphere on the earth, thus suddenly braking its rotation. This, in turn, might trigger massive earthquakes in areas where the crust has developed instability. Scientists already possess evidence that solar activity affects the nature and severity of earthquakes.

To these newest threats to mother earth we might add an inherited list from previous prognosticators. Far in the distant future, one group of scientists suggests, we face a cooling process that will slowly freeze life off the earth. Not so, another group counters;

the sun will explode and fry the world free of life. One French scientist offered a bizarre climax. Earth, he claims, will continue to bear an increasing burden of human life. Resources will enable populations to increase indefinitely. Keeping man cool from his own heat will finally bring the end of life. Layers of multilevel housing units will cover every square inch of the earth and give off storms of heat from air-conditioning systems. At its finale mankind will virtually cook itself to death.

While these predictions may offer something a little more believable than the Children of God's guess that the comet Kohoutek would destroy life, they hardly give much more comfort.

Prophecies that push the end of the earth off into the far future don't mean too much right now, but what of the other concepts that bring it closer, even within a lifetime?

With such a terrifying future ahead and this earth itself wracked with insuperable problems, it isn't hard to join those who suggest that the best hope for mankind would be to go somewhere else, find another planet, search the stars for another home.

Such an idea isn't all that new. One doesn't have to read very far in the New Testament before the great hope of Christians appears. That "blessed hope" includes leaving Earth for another, better, safer place.

Many Bible students have nurtured their expectations on an invasion-from-space attitude toward the Second Coming, forgetting that the coming is to take God's people away from planet Earth. But when you examine the Bible, you sense an urgency in the longings for the return of Christ. The Bible writers see a world in trouble, they know Christ as the solution, they want Him back soon to set things right, and, finally, they want to go with Him to the place prepared.

After John had seen the playback of the last generations of Earth, he wrote this: "He who gives this testimony speaks: 'Yes, I am coming soon!' Amen. Come, Lord Jesus!" (Revelation 22:20, NEB). Jesus delineated the unsuitability of Earth's conditions for His people and told His disciples, " 'There are many dwelling-places in my Father's house; if it were not so I should have told you; for I am going there on purpose to prepare a place for you. And if I go and prepare a place for you, I shall come again and receive you to myself' " (John 14:2, 3, NEB).

Though the happy thought of being with the Master through all ages spurs anticipation of His return, the concept of deliverance from a spoiled world permeates Christian teaching. " 'It will be a time of great distress; there has never been such a time from the beginning of the world until now, and will never be again. If that time of troubles were not cut short, no living thing could survive; but for the sake of God's chosen it will be cut short' " (Matthew 24:21, 22, NEB).

God never permits the spiritual or physical environment to produce conditions impossible for His people to survive. He does say, however, that when that time comes, He will take His people away from earth.

Christians living at the time of the destruction of Jerusalem saw this prophecy fulfilled for them in their sudden and unexpected escape from Titus' armies. Reformation and post-Reformation expositors viewed the oppression and persecution of the Dark and Middle Ages as a fulfillment of this prophecy and saw escape in the stand of Luther, Calvin, Knox, and other Reformers who forced back the overwhelming power of the Papacy.

In our age we have seen physical deterioration of man's ecology join with spiritual degradation in threatening the survival of Christians both in spirit and in body. The global nature of the threat reinforces escape from this earth as the solution.

Modern theologians grapple with the problems of making theology fit social and ecological conditions. Social concern, participation in drives to control garbage piles, and activism in political events all reflect the new theology.

Jürgen Mottmann, one conductor of the theological orchestra, is suggesting that Christians join him in a "theology of hope." He dares to propose that the fulfillment of Christian ideals will come through Christianity's fusing with communism to force a new faith, a new society. The history of politics as an aid to Christian belief reeks with excesses and tragedies. Yet the theology of hope presumes that the magic of Marxian theology (if that is not a basic contradiction of terms to start with) will march us all down the road to a new world.

Not every one of Mottmann's followers concurs in all his dreams. But if the theology of today presages the belief of tomorrow, we may well expect a revival of the Augustinian millennialism that filled the 1920's and 30's with rosy but unrealistic predictions of man's progress toward a self-regulated Utopia.

The Bible's insistence on escape underlines the Thessalonian solution: "Because at the word of command, at the sound of the archangel's voice and God's trumpet-call, the Lord himself will descend from heaven; first the Christian dead will rise, then we who are left alive shall join them, caught up in clouds to meet the Lord in the air. Thus we shall always be with the Lord" (1 Thessalonians 4:16, 17, NEB). In considering the confusion that Satan will produce in the last days, Paul calls the coming of our Lord Jesus Christ a "gathering of us to himself" (2 Thessalonians 2:1, NEB). Always the movement of God's people is upward and away from a devastated society, a disintegrating earth.

Peter presents a planetwide pyre that accomplishes two ends. It preserves a people and re-creates an environment. "But the Day of the Lord will come; it will come unexpected as a thief. On that day the heavens will disappear with a great rushing sound, the elements will disintegrate in flames, and the earth with all that is in it will be laid bare. . . . That day will set the heavens ablaze until they fall apart, and will melt the elements in flames. But we have his promise, and look forward to new heavens and a new earth, the home of justice" (2 Peter 3:10-13, NEB).

The visions of the Apocalypse present a last-day scene from which the only escape is away. Consider the ecology of the Second Coming: "And there was a violent earthquake; the sun turned black as a funeral pall and the moon all red as blood; the stars in the sky fell to the earth, like figs shaken down by a gale; the sky vanished, as a scroll is rolled up, and every mountain and island was moved from its place" (Revelation 6:12-14, NEB).

Those not orbited away at the coming of Christ

will see only one advantage in the chaos: "Then the kings of the earth, magnates and marshals, the rich and the powerful, and all men, slave or free, hid themselves in caves and mountain crags; and they called out to the mountains and the crags, 'Fall on us and hide us from the face of the One who sits on the throne and from the vengeance of the Lamb' " (verses 15, 16, NEB).

Justice reacts against those who have decimated society; it is a "time to destroy those who destroy the earth" (Revelation 11:18, NEB). This God does by declaring ecological warfare against the culpable. One by one the plagues itemize and epitomize the counts against those responsible for the condition of the earth. Antichrist has declared an identification program that separates his cohorts from the followers of the Lamb. The plagues stigmatize his hierarchy with incurable sores (Revelation 16).

Profligate society has fouled the ocean into a cesspool, and now, despite endeavors to reverse the process, the sea turns into a putrid, bloody tide. The streams that environmentalists have fought to make drinkable, flow as red as if man had knifed deep wounds into nature's side.

Retribution for greed? Yes, and more. Punishment for persecution. "They shed the blood of thy people and of thy prophets, and thou hast given them blood to drink. They have their deserts!" (Revelation 16:6, NEB).

In a two-thousand-year-old portrayal of what might happen with the dissipation of the ozone layer, the plagues continue: "The fourth angel poured his bowl on the sun; and it was allowed to burn men with its flames. They were fearfully burned; but they only cursed the name of God who had the power to inflict such plagues, and they refused to repent or to do him homage" (Revelation 16:8, 9, NEB).

In the seventh plague God manipulates the atmosphere and geophysical forces to produce the final upheaval. This, following the intense darkness and climactic war of the fifth and sixth plagues and the destroying fire of the presence of Christ, obliterates humanity from the earth. Only those who have escaped to the care of the Deliverer survive.

Now comes the time of renewal. A desolate earth rests, awaiting the moment of re-creation. "I saw the earth, and it was without form and void; the heavens, and their light was gone. I saw the mountains, and they reeled; all the hills rocked to and fro. I saw, and there was no man, and the very birds had taken flight. I saw, and the farm-land was wilderness, and the towns all razed to the ground, before the Lord in his anger. These are the words of the Lord: The whole land shall be desolate, though I will not make an end of it" (Jeremiah 4:23-27, NEB).

With such a Biblical view, Christians accept the extrapolations of scientists. The earth will end in a cosmic disaster. While its people sense omens of cataclysm, God defines the event and delineates the causes. Yet God pushes the future beyond the end of the world and remakes our planet. While the wise men of earth scrabble for alternates to the rollercoaster ride on which humanity launched itself at the moment of the first transgression, God has His own plans for preserving a people to inherit the good and beautiful earth of tomorrow.

Curators tell us that the Tower of Pisa continues to lean farther and farther away from the perpendicular. Someday, perhaps in a few years, it will lean too far and collapse into rubble. A modern tower of Babel builds on foundations of exploitation, disbelief, self-sufficiency, and presumption. The discerning eye watches it lean farther and farther toward collapse. The eye of faith and the eye of science both sense the impending crash. The question has long since proceeded past an "if" to a "when?"

But there is a phoenix in our future. Out of the fires of the last days a new world arises, "wherein dwelleth righteousness." It has its own ecology, its own protective devices, and because it is peopled with the new race of the redeemed, the threat of repeated evil does not exist.

This is the environment where the wolf and the lamb lie down together; where vineyards are for the enjoyment of the people, not the enrichment of the landlord; where the sun offers no harm; where the Sahel becomes a garden; where "none shall make them afraid."

So many ways to end the world, but only one offers hope for a new world. And as the Bible declares, "The time is at hand" (Revelation 22:10, KJV).

How Many People Will God Save?

The sound of bells, of trotting oxen, of laughter and chanting, woke us long before dawn. From the hotel window we could see streams of people flowing like a tributary toward Mother Ganges. Today they would worship the sun, and all Patna stirred to the stimuli of the Hindus' routine of festival.

Baskets bore gifts of food and fruit to be held aloft to the sun's first rays and then taken home for a ritual meal. Tiny oil lamps flickered in wicker containers; soon they would float in a twinkling armada on the bosom of the river.

The impression of people, people, people, intensified as we pushed our way to the riverbank and looked back at the hosts moving to the water. Every available inch of the ghats held a devotee, eyes straining for the first glimpse of the sun. At river's edge men and women dipped themselves in purification rites as the sun peered above the eastern bank.

If ever the millions of the unsaved press upon the Christian, it is when witnessing pagan rites. Everything so wrong, so different, and how does one change it? How does the gospel break through?

And while one stands and watches, the numbers grow and grow and the questions multiply. How many people does God want saved? When will His work be done? When can we say the gospel has been preached to the ends of the world for the witness it must give?

Sometimes the thought surfaces that God must be interested in saving large numbers of people; sometimes it seems that He searches for a spiritual elite.

God had no ideas of a small number or empty spaces when He made Adam and Eve. "God blessed them and said to them, 'Be fruitful and increase, fill the earth and subdue it, rule over the fish in the sea, the birds of heaven, and every living thing that moves upon the earth' " (Genesis 1:28, NEB). God wanted an earth full of humans, a paradise of people that would replicate Eden away to the very corners of the globe.

Perhaps all the sons of God shouted for joy because they saw this potential. They looked for the planet to fill with descendants of the first pair. They anticipated the communion and contribution of this earth as it entered fully into the bountiful variety of the universe. They agreed with God that it was indeed "good." It gave cause for rejoicing, for those songs and shouts of joy, that the Bible tells us heralded the new world.

When sin came, God immediately removed the threat of a world peopled with immortal sinners. Blocking access to the tree of life, He reminded Adam and Eve of the fate they must face. They would die, but their children would increase.

How narrowly God averted complete annihilation of His creation may be judged from the eight that survived the Flood. Despite proximity to Creation and to the Garden of Eden the number of God's people sank to a nadir as Noah preached his fruitless 120 years.

God's patience with the antediluvians shows the optimism of divinity. God is the Father of optimism. He thinks thoughts of love, thoughts of success. He waits and hopes. "It is not that the Lord is slow in fulfilling his promise, as some suppose, but that he is very patient with you, because it is not his will for any to be lost, but for all to come to repentance" (2 Peter 3:9, NEB).

After the Flood demonstrated that God could not tolerate a race that moved constantly against Him, intent on believing Satan's seductions rather than God's commands, God set in motion a plan that still carries today. Searching the earth for a faithful heart, He found Abram and told him that he would become the progenitor of a nation of believers in God.

He offered Abram and Sarai fabulous dreams: "I will make you into a great nation, I will bless you and make your name so great that it shall be used in blessings" (Genesis 12:2, NEB).

"I will make your descendants countless as the dust of the earth; if anyone could count the dust upon the ground, then he could count your descendants" (Genesis 13:16, NEB).

" 'Look up into the sky, and count the stars if you can. So many', he said, 'shall your descendants be' " (Genesis 15:5, NEB).

Abram dubbed God's prophecy a dream but loved the dream so much that he tried to help God by taking Hagar as wife. Sarai thought it all ridiculous;

certainly God was no gynecologist or He would not talk so, and she laughed. But all this changed, and Abraham became the father of the faithful.

Right there God reiterated what He had told Adam and Eve—His plan to fill the earth with His children, sons and daughters of God. Israel expected it through national conquest. God finally showed that the battles to be won are spiritual and that the faithful will come from all nations.

But the story has another element. For hundreds of years Israel teeter-tottered its way toward destiny. At times it looked like the Israelites might become the spiritual saviors of the world. But often those who reveled in the shrines and groves outnumbered those who brought sacrifices to the Temple in Jerusalem. In the frustration of human perversity the prophets begin to speak of a remnant.

Elijah strives and conquers on Mount Carmel and then accuses God of failure because he considers himself the only faithful one left in the entire nation. God rebukes him and tells him of seven thousand more, the faithful remnant.

The northern kingdom scatters and dies in the Assyrian domain. Judah follows into the Babylonian provinces, and the prophets talk of the remnant that will return and will reestablish Jerusalem.

"Then everyone who invokes the Lord by name shall be saved; for when the Lord gives the word there shall yet be survivors on Mount Zion and in Jerusalem a remnant whom the Lord will call" (Joel 2:32, NEB).

Survival seems a far cry from "the dust of the ground" and "the stars of the sky." Yet God still will not be denied.

These very words of the prophet Joel became the *raison d'être* of the early church. Faced with the conversion explosion of Pentecost, Peter explained to the people what was happening; "for the promise is to you, and to your children, and to all who are far away, everyone whom the Lord our God may call" (Acts 2:39, NEB).

Paul, facing the puzzling question of whether all would hear the story of salvation, sealed his argument by quoting from Joel 2:32: "For everyone, as it says again—'everyone who invokes the name of the Lord will be saved'" (Romans 10:13, NEB).

The gospel presents the same dichotomy as the Old Testament. On the one hand Jesus commands the gospel to all people everywhere; on the other hand concepts of the remnant persist. Yet God did not intend that the remnant idea should stall the spread of the gospel.

My father tells of the time when the membership of the Seventh-day Adventist Church was creeping toward the mystery number of Revelation, 144,000. For years many had been nurtured in the belief that God would save only that many people when Christ returned. And now the "remnant church" was approaching that number. Perhaps when the counter ticked past a gross of thousands, probation would close or the latter rain would fall.

But the statistics moved steadily on. They thought again. How foolish of them! It couldn't be 144,000; it had to be 288,000 adherents! After all the Bible does say "one shall be taken, and the other left." To make up 144,000 one had to have 288,000 to start with!

How many is a remnant? Two concepts run along with the word *remnant*. We are familiar with the idea of smallness. A woman goes to the remnant counter and rummages among lengths of cloth that are too small for a dress and too large for a blouse —that's a remnant. But there is also the concept of a part left over from a former entity—carrying the characteristics of the other but continuing to exist with those characteristics.

God has no thoughts of a handful when one comes to the last book of the Bible. John looks into heaven and sees that "a great multitude, which no man could number, of all nations, and kindreds, and people, and tongues, stood before the throne, and before the Lamb, clothed with white robes, and palms in their hands" (Revelation 7:9, KJV).

Where did this multitude originate? True, it represents all the faithful of all ages. But let us remember that only in our age have all nations been included; the gospel to the world in the fullest sense belongs to the past one hundred years. So while a modular sense moves vertically through time with blocks of people eligible for God's kingdom from all the eras of the past, only in our day could the horizontal module be meaningful and modules from all nations be included among the redeemed.

The angel of Revelation 14:6 announces the new era of mass communication: "Then I saw an angel flying in mid-heaven, with an eternal gospel to proclaim to those on earth, to every nation and tribe, language and people" (NEB). Success comes to the spread of this message, for a few verses later another angel states, "*Here* is the patience of the saints: *here* are they that keep the commandments of God, and the faith of Jesus" (Revelation 14:12, KJV). Where was the angel looking when he said "here"? Tokyo?

Washington, D.C.? Sydney? São Paulo? Wagga Wagga? Loma Linda? With a globe-girdling sweep of his finger he said of everywhere, "Here are they."

The second of Satan's great wars against God is directed especially against the "remnant." Great War I ended in defeat for the devil. Michael cast him out of heaven. In that battle God succeeded in saving two thirds of the angels. Can we expect that the Lord will walk away from Great War II with a handful of survivors? "And the dragon was wroth with the woman, and went to make war with the remnant of her seed, which keep the commandments of God, and have the testimony of Jesus Christ" (Revelation 12:17, KJV). Does this remnant refer to numbers or continuity? Is it quantity of people or quality of belief that determines Satan's antagonists?

The concern of prophecy isn't with the number who "keep the commandments of God." It's with the seed of the woman, the spiritual heirs of the apostolic church. Purity of belief holds far more meaning than the counting of their number.

Revelation 12 tells the story of the establishment of the pattern of truth, woven by the life of Jesus and deeds and teachings of the apostles. It tells of Satan's furious war against the truth and those who preserved truth. The miracle of the preservation of the fabric of truth occurs as the church flies to the wilderness to escape the weakened fibers and bizarre designs Satan seeks to insert into the pattern. Then the remnant appears. Not as a snippet of the original cloth, but as part of the same true pattern, the same quality of belief.

God wants quality of belief rather than quantity of numbers.

Yet this is not to say that the numbers will be small. Far from it. With four billion potential followers of the Lamb the future opens immense possibilities of success.

The direction of truth remains constant, both in content and in the lives of those who cherish it. It leads toward God and His kingdom. Those who accept this truth see their neighbor and the whole world with the same optimism with which Heaven regards us. They see each person as potential for the kingdom. They see that all men can be woven as part of the pattern of truth, all men can share in the victory of the remnant. They do not attempt to number the "great multitude"; they seek to swell it.

Thus the God who will not be thwarted brings His plans to climax. For countless millions the direction of life will find its destination in the presence of God Himself. The Godward flow started by the current of Calvary will draw and pull upon the hearts and consciences of men until God has His "dust of the ground" and "stars of the sky," and the earth is replenished with His new people.